Life Can Begin Again

Take God out of the universe and everything is annihilated, every higher joy of the mind, every love, and only the wish for mental suicide would remain, and only the devil and the beast would still desire to exist.

—Jean Paul Richter, *Dream of a World without God*

I have not done what God desired of me; that is certain. On the contrary, I have only dreamed of what I wanted from God. . . . —Léon Bloy, *Last Journals*

LIFE CAN BEGIN AGAIN

SERMONS ON THE SERMON ON THE MOUNT

By Helmut Thielicke

translated by John W. Doberstein

FORTRESS PRESS   PHILADELPHIA

This book is a translation from *Das Leben kann noch einmal beginnen. Ein Gang durch die Bergpredigt* (4th rev. ed.; Stuttgart: Quell-Verlag, 1958). Copyright Quell-Verlag, 1956.

To my friends

at

Drew University, Madison, New Jersey

Translator's Note

This book is the last of a great quartet of "series sermons" on some central, familiar biblical materials: in the order of their appearance in English the parables of Jesus, the Lord's Prayer, the first chapters of Genesis, and now the Sermon on the Mount. In many ways this volume may prove to be the most valuable of them all, for the Sermon on the Mount is so commonly misinterpreted as a collection of lovely, impossible ideals. Helmut Thielicke makes it clear in every chapter that the Sermon on the Mount can never be understood, indeed, will always be misunderstood, if even for a moment we forget the Preacher of the Sermon. For apart from the person and work of Jesus Christ these marvelous words are the most radical and devastating distillation of God's claims that it is possible to conceive; they leave us in utter, hopeless dismay. Only "in Christ" do these words of the law become the glorious gospel that promises that for every man "life can begin again." The last sermon in this book achieves a compelling beauty which even the hazards and ineptitudes of translation cannot wholly obscure. Again the translator is happy to have a part in helping this great preacher to tell us in our own tongue the mighty works of God.

Mount Airy, Philadelphia   John W. Doberstein
January, 1963

Contents

To the Reader

The real trouble of modern man expresses itself in two kinds of fear: fear of the past and fear of the future.

Fear of the *past* has been a repeated theme of the existentialists. How can I ever get away from all that lies behind me, the points where I made decisions, right or wrong, but in any case unalterable, which now determine my life? How can I get away from the guilt that lies behind me and now can never be undone? For time is like a one-way street that leads me to the future and never allows me to turn back to the past stations of my life and make revisions. Therefore I am in the grip of my past and I cannot undo it. I am the prisoner of my own past, and the past is dreadfully irreversible. It determines me and makes an object of me. How can I ever disentangle myself from this net of the past perfect? How can I get the reins of my life into my hands again and guide the steeds according to my will, instead of helplessly hanging on to the reins and being dragged around by these unbridled horses? How numerous the dramas of our time in which this question is the *cantus firmus*, and how we prick up our ears when this theme of life and the anxiety of life is struck!

But my relationship to the *future* is also broken. The time is past when men composed shining utopias in which technology and social justice seemed about to lead humanity to paradise regained. "The future has already begun." But on its threshold no joyful bells appear to be ringing; we hear only the scream of sirens. Quite obviously we are not sailing into peaceful harbors; on the contrary, we see ourselves becoming ensnared in deadly adventures and nobody knows how it will turn out. If at this moment we are not exactly saying, "Tarry a while (hold up the future for a moment longer!) thou art so fair," we still live by the motto, "If the world ends tomorrow, today is today."

What we need and what we yearn for is something that will liberate us from paralysis and help us gain a new attitude toward what lies behind us and ahead of us.

This yearning for some real help with which to face life is met by the Sermon on the Mount, or better, by the Proclaimer of the Sermon on the Mount himself. Only at first glance could it appear that here we are being pelted with a great profusion of directions and imperatives, often piercingly radical in their demands. And yet I must immediately correct myself: it is perfectly true to say they are "piercingly radical." Here there is no talk of half measures and compromises, and anybody who merely wants to play around with it had better let it alone. Here it is all or nothing. And yet the term "piercing radicality" does not express the essential point; for other people have been radical too. Anybody who knows Kant the ethicist and his categorical imperative knows that his radicality can hardly be surpassed. With all the skill of a sharp-witted sleuth he ferrets out man in every secret hole in which he seeks a refuge where he can be alone with his urges and his furious thirst for happiness and power of prestige. And how about the fanatics of every age, the respectable people whose "purity it was to will one thing" (Kierkegaard), who with a manic obsession and yet with an incomparable devotion subordinated everything to the *one* goal which they thought was right, regardless of losses and letting nothing stand in their way?

We moderns are for the most part activists. We live by our will, and we accept the principle that "if it does not kill me it will cure me." It may be the dim suspicion that this motivation only makes us whirl ever faster on the carousel of a vicious circle that causes us to respond to appeals to the will with a certain resignation and view all radicalisms with a bit of skepticism. After all, was it not the great men of fanatical will, the "terrible simplifiers" (the *terribles simplificateurs*) who led us into the abyss?

Therefore, in the Sermon on the Mount we should consider less the piercing radicality of its directions and give more consideration to the Figure who is speaking here and has a definite purpose in view when he speaks in these radical terms. What is this ultimate thing?

Well, whatever it may be—and we shall attempt to learn what it is—there is one thing that we must take cognizance of in these first pages and that is that we are not given something to do without first being given something. And this really is different from what we hear from Kant and the other rigorists. Here it is not demanded that we free ourselves from our past by sheer force and a titanic effort of will and simply begin a new life. This would only put us back on the rack again and besides, it would be illusionary.

> He who into the future leaps
> Goes down to ruin.
> And whether the leap success or failure reaps,
> The man who leaps
> Goes down to ruin.
>
> —*Erich Kästner*

The Sermon on the Mount is uttered against a wholly different background. The Proclaimer of the Sermon on the Mount says to us: before you begin intelligently to strike out on a new path and make a fresh start on life, you must first realize that everything that lies behind you has been set straight, that someone else has taken on your burdens, and that now you can really begin your new life—to use a phrase of Anouilh which he used with a wholly different connotation—as a "traveler without luggage."

And yet there is something else that must be made clear at the outset. The radical, straight, earnest road to which we are directed, the entrance to which is a very narrow gate, is not so laid out that it will "lead" us into a new future. In nonfigurative language, the radicality of the demands is not intended to force a new situation in humanity and personal life by whipping up, as it were, an increased intensity of zeal and determination. No, what the Sermon on the Mount sets forth is not the kind of dream that Kant, and also the fanatics in their way, dreamed. On the contrary, instead of fostering the illusion that we can bring about a new world situation and a new future by a radical exertion of the will, the Sermon on the Mount says to us: a future has been *given* to you, the air is full of promises, the ship of your life and history itself is sailing toward a harbor where you are expected and your safety assured. You are still pitching upon the hazardous waves, and hurricanes roar and strike terror in your hearts. But something has happened that will bring all your ways and wanderings to this goal, that will cause a future prepared for you in grace to come upon you. The future has already begun—but how different that sounds in the Sermon on the Mount; how marvelously dread has been changed into assurance! What is the future that is meant here? Again this is what we shall try to find out in this book.

In any case, because this future has already begun we can live in it; we are no longer absorbed by the present moment and the old monotonous routine of workdays and Sundays. In the name of that future we can afford to be radical and absolutely straight, without allowing ourselves to be pushed off on the diagonals of the parallelogram of power or to tack on a zigzag course. In other words: first comes the future and then the unconditional demand, the straight line, the right course—and not the other way around.

Is it worth while to listen to this message? It does not say: you *must* begin a new life! As if we could do such a thing anyhow, as if we were even willing to *listen* to such a thing! What it says is: something has happened in the province of life and you must allow it to give its signal to you. And then because that signal has been given, you can start afresh; life can begin again. There are, of course, some very definite directions for this new life. But first there are some things that are simply *given* to us and we must accept them. To be able to begin afresh, to become a "traveler without luggage"—this itself is incredibly new; and if it is to be possible, it will require a miracle. And as a matter of fact, it is the purpose of this book to tell about a miracle and to ask the question of how then one can live on the strength of that miracle.

With regard to the origin and fortune of this book, there is this to be said. It is the fourth edition of a collection of addresses on the Sermon on the Mount which the author delivered in St. Mark's Church in Stuttgart during the worst of the postwar years, 1946-1948. The individual chapters have been thoroughly revised. References to definite events and conditions prevailing at the time when they were first delivered which would no longer be understood or which have lost their interest, have been eliminated. Nevertheless, here and there I have allowed something of the coloration of the time to remain (for example, in chapter eleven); for in more than one respect that time had in it something that was profoundly typical of man's *Anfechtung*, temptation, despair, and need. It was a boundary situation in which—humanly speaking—man's flank was often more exposed to and less fortified against the Word of God than in more normal times. We ought to go back to this chapter of our own life occasionally whenever we find it hard to hear the Word of God.

1

Journey Without Luggage

And he came down with them and stood on a level place, with a
great crowd of his disciples and a great multitude of people from
all Judea and Jerusalem and the seacoast of Tyre and Sidon, who
came to hear him and to be healed of their diseases; and those who
were troubled with unclean spirits were cured. And all the crowd
sought to touch him, for power came forth from him and healed
them all.

And he lifted up his eyes on his disciples, and said:

"Blessed are you poor, for yours is the kingdom of God.

"Blessed are you that hunger now, for you shall be satisfied.

"Blessed are you that weep now, for you shall laugh."

—Luke 6:17-21 (cf. Matthew 5:1-9)

When Jesus had taken his place and saw the great crowd of
people gathered around him he began to read what he saw in the
multitude of eyes directed at him.

What was written in those eyes?

It was probably a mingling of hope and fear, of anxiety and
covert expectation.

To begin with, there was the host of the miserable, the guilt-
burdened, the lonely, the incurably ill, the careworn, the people
who were hagridden by anxiety. They gaze at him with inscrutable eyes that can be fathomed only by the Savior himself.

Normally, we never see the miserable gathered together in this
way. Suffering and sorrow usually creep away and hide themselves.

Just suppose that suddenly all the hospitals and asylums were emptied. Could we bear the sight of the crippled and mutilated, the pallor of death, the hopelessness? Could we bear to listen to the shrill cacophony of mumbling, babbling, lunatic voices, the shrieks of people tormented by persecution delusions and demonic possession?

So all these miserable, burdened people are gathered here around Jesus; for in some mysterious way Jesus attracts the miserable. He draws the sinners and sufferers from their hiding places like a magnet. Undoubtedly, the reason for this is that men sense in this Figure something they do not see in any other man.

For one thing they see (and we all see) that he stands among us as if he were one of us; he stands the test of misery. He does not act as do the influential "upper ten thousand" of this world, who build exclusive residential districts where they cannot see the world's misery, who send a monthly check to an institution for the destitute, but whom ten horses could not drag to the place where they would prefer to send their unfeeling money by itself. They are afraid to expose their hearts or even their nerves to all this. They fear that their Persian rugs would begin to burn beneath their feet and they would no longer get any pleasure out of them. They are afraid that their gleaming chandeliers would no longer be able to sweep away from their eyes the darkness they would have to gaze into there.

So these people are grateful to the Savior for coming to their miserable slum, grateful that he does not close his eyes as the vast army of those who are shadowed by suffering passes by.

At the same time, however, they see in him something else, which is far more incomprehensible and, put alongside of their first observation, almost inconceivable: the fact that the powers of guilt and suffering cannot touch him, that, mysteriously, these powers retreat as he comes by. To be sure, his heart, too, shuddered beneath the onslaughts of hell in the wilderness; for, after all, it was his will to possess a human heart, to which nothing human, no temptation, no dread, is alien. But sullen Satan was defeated and left the arena without having accomplished anything whatsoever. The same thing happened on the Cross. There, too, he was clutched and clawed by physical pain and the dread of dereliction; but again his spirit burst through the deadly encirclement and found the way to the Father's hand.

So they all sought to get near to him. They gazed with wistful longing at his hands that could do so much good and never wearied of blessing and healing.

But now his hands were at rest. Now he seated himself and began to speak.

We wonder whether they were not a little, perhaps even greatly, disappointed. People generally prefer "practical Christianity, the religion of action." They would much rather have him satisfy their hunger, bind up their wounds, and drive the mad fear from their minds.

But here he is opening his mouth to speak. Why does he turn to speech when all this misery cries out for action? Now, these people think, now come the theories and the doctrines that never feed and heal a man, that never warm a man's bones, that never bring back a dead son, never fill the dread emptiness of the future.

But even more: perhaps what he says will only make us more sick than we were before. Haven't people always been claiming that this is so? All respect to practical brotherly love! But have not the "dogmas" of Christianity brought miseries upon miseries to the world? Hasn't it constantly been creating separations between people? Hasn't it broken up communities, unleashed wars, troubled consciences, and robbed us of peace of mind?

So these people here may be thinking too. What will he have to say?

Probably what everybody already knows anyhow: that the misery and suffering gathered there before him represents a *judgment*, that the whole creation is corrupt, and so on. Oh, we know that old story of the preachers!

At any rate he'll be calling us to repentance, as John the Baptist did not long ago. He won't have anything else to say except to go on repeating with painful monotony: The ax is laid to the root of the trees and the Last Judgment is near.

These people who are gathered around Jesus know, or at least think they know, what is coming when Jesus opens his mouth: God's declaration of war against man, denunciation of sin, painful, scrutinizing exposure of those innermost thoughts with which God is not pleased.

The preachers are always beating this same old track. Everybody knows this. These people know precisely what is coming. And this in itself is very distressing and tiresome. Nor will they be able to contradict it, for this preacher of penitence from Nazareth is certainly right. But this only makes it more painful and depressing. That stuff never gets you anywhere. Nobody is helped by negatives, even when they are true.

Then Jesus opened his mouth and something completely unexpected happened, something that drove these people to an astonishment bordering upon terror, something that held them spellbound long after he ceased speaking and would not let them rest. Jesus said to the people gathered around him, people who were harried by suffering, misery, and guilt: "Blessed are you; blessed are you." The Sermon on the Mount closes with the remark that the crowds were astonished and frightened, even though it was a sermon on grace. But this is what always happens when God unveils his great goodness. It is so immense, so far beyond and contrary to all human dimensions and conceptions that at first one simply cannot understand it and we stand there in utter helpless bewilderment. The shepherds at Christmas were also unable at first to exult over the great light that broke through the darkness over the earth but could only fall to their knees in fear and scurry for cover.

When Jesus preached repentance, when Jesus wept over Jerusalem, which even then would not recognize the things that make for peace, he did so in a voice almost choked with tears. How is it that the language of the Bible, which is normally so strong and unsentimental, should at this point speak of tears? Jesus wept not only because these were *his* people who were lurching so unavertibly toward the abyss. No, Jesus wept because he knew the power of the Seducer, the menacing mystery of the devil, who seizes even the upright, the respectable, the morally intact people by the throat, and grips them in such a way that at first even they themselves (if they do not have the gift of distinguishing between spirits) have no premonition of the dreadful slopes to which they are being edged by a consummate cunning.

This is, after all, the ghastly mystery of the terrible twelve years in which we were dealing with this dark power in Germany, years in which the devil proved himself to be a master of every ruse and camouflage. In those years that lie behind us he did not appeal to the *base* instincts of our people, but challenged the sacrificial spirit and devotion of men. He caught hold of youth at the point of their idealism and their love for their country and, posing as an angel of light, played his diabolical games with the best attributes of our people.

Only because Jesus knew this power of the Seducer and because he grieved over those who were being seduced are we brought to the point where he wrests from our hearts the innermost willingness to *accept* judgment from *him*.

This is rather an amazing thing. For can there be any harsher judgment than that of the Cross of Golgotha, surrounded not only by the hangman's myrmidons and the masses roused to the pitch of sadism, but also by the best and most moral examples of humanity? And yet all of them together constitute a chorus, giving appalling expression to megalomania, their vanity, and their bad conscience. The fact is that we are all represented in that furious mob around the Cross. "Mine, mine was the transgression, But thine the deadly pain."

And yet we accept this judgment that comes from Golgotha. Simply because we sense that here a man died for those whom he himself would have to accuse, that here a man gave his life for those who have forfeited their lives, that here a man stood at bay, in his own flesh and blood, and therefore in an ultimate comradeship with us all, against the powers that would torment and destroy us.

The hard judgments which the Sermon on the Mount hurls upon us all, relentlessly unmasking the deepest secrets and urges of our hearts, are spoken by a Savior who in the very midst of judgment calls out to us "Blessed are you," a Savior who does not only fling out the cry "Woe to you," but invites us to the Father's house. These judgments are spoken by a Savior whose hand is not clenched into a smashing, repulsing fist, but is opened in the gesture of blessing, and as he blesses we see the wounds he suffered for our sake.

This leads us to the second point at which the utter difference between the judgments of God and the way in which we men are accustomed to judge and condemn becomes clear.

No man has ever yet been healed by judgment and punishment. Always the merely negative only makes us sick. What good does it do if in the midst of the judgment and retribution that comes to us we must say it serves you right; you can't kick; you made your bed and now you must lie in it.

I ask: What good does it do to have this insight into judgment? Obviously, none at all. It only pitches us into deeper hopelessness and inner paralysis, and in not a few people stirs up the horrible and sinful desire to end it all by violence.

The judgment by itself is no help at all if there is nothing else besides. Therefore God too is never the judge, but always, in the midst of judgment and in the midst of personal, vocational, and family catastrophe, he is the seeking God, the God who is seeking to bring us home, the "Savior," the restoring God. God is always positive, even in the very worst of the judgments and terrors that he must permit to come upon us.

That's how the beatitudes are to be understood: a hand stretched out to us in the midst of suffering and care, a hand that makes it clear that God still has a design for us and that he wants to lead us to goals so lovely that we shall weep for joy. God never merely stops with our past, though he does not let us get away with anything and puts his finger upon our sorest wounds. He is always the Lord who is concerned about our future, paving the way to save us and guiding us to his goals.

If we really want to learn to evaluate and rejoice in this positive side of judgment and be able to reach out for it in every time of need and suffering we shall have to guard against two misconceptions.

The *first* is this. We all know that familiar saying of Goethe: "Blessed is he that cuts himself off from the world without hatred. . . ." All of us have gone through hard, desperate, fear-scourged, hopeless hours of life, times in which we have tried to escape on the wings of dreams to some region where, to use Adalbert Stifter's phrase, the "gentle law" still reigns. At such times older folks may dream of the days of their youth when things were different and youth may dream of a future when things will be different. But is that true blessedness, true happiness? Isn't it only a shot of morphine that makes us dependent and unfit and only throws us back more helplessly into hard reality?

Jesus says something altogether different to us in his beatitudes. For he addresses his call specifically to those who are in a predicament, the poor, those who are suffering because of their own shortcomings and failures, the guilty, the grieving, the persecuted, the hungry and thirsty. Why should he call these, of all people, blessed? Is this merely cruel irony? What would someone who had been told yesterday by the doctor that he was suffering from cancer say if you called him "blessed"? What would a woman who had been betrayed by her husband and robbed of her dignity say? Or a mother who sees her child going wrong? Or a young man who lives in desperate loneliness in a rented room somewhere in a big city?

Isn't it sheer mockery to call these people "blessed"—whether in Goethe's sense or even in the sense of Jesus of Nazareth?

But now, listen to this.

When we are dealing with the beatitudes of Jesus, we must not leave out of account *him* who spoke them; we dare not assess them as sentences or maxims of a general philosophy of life which are to be measured by whatever truth they contain within themselves.

In all of these utterances Jesus is secretly pointing to himself. And if we hear them addressed to us today by him who has been exalted to the right hand of power and looks down upon us from the glory of his eternity, then this is what he is saying to us:

"The first reason why you who are miserable and afraid are to be called blessed is simply because *I* am in the midst of you. You complain because you must suffer? Look, I myself found my real mission and learned obedience in what I suffered. You complain because you have to drink a bitter cup? Look, when I myself was compelled to drink the most ghastly draught any man ever faced I learned to say, 'Not my will, but thine, be done.' So I found peace in unconditional acceptance of the will of my Father. You complain that in all your sufferings the face of God has vanished, that you cannot feel his presence at all, and you are left so dreadfully alone? Look, *I* too had that feeling of Godforsakenness; it found its vent in that terrible cry of dereliction, and the sun was darkened because it could not bear the extremity of that loneliness. But while my tortured body drooped, but was held and could not fall because of the burning nails, suddenly the Father's hand was there beneath me to break my fall and snatch my spirit from the anguish.

"Don't you understand this, my brothers? The first beatitude is that *I* am in the midst of you and that, because you are suffering my sorrows, I will also lead you to my fulfillments and my blessings."

Then the *second* reason for blessedness.

We should not think that Jesus merely wanted to give us a few maxims of practical wisdom, that he merely intended to talk about the blessing of suffering and poverty and console us by telling us that suffering would make us more mature. Jesus knew all too well that it can turn out just the opposite, that a man can break down under suffering, that it can drive us into cursing instead of prayer, and that its ultimate effect will perhaps be bitter complaining and accusing of God for his injustice.

No, because it is *he* who is present, because he is in the midst of us, he comes not as a teacher but as the Savior. These are not just words, words, words; something *happens* to us.

For now we have a signature, sealed with blood and sanctified by the Savior's sufferings, declaring that heaven has been opened to us, even when everything around us is locked tight, even if there should never again be any improvement, any future, any merriment or laughter in our lives. We have the signature which certifies that "in *everything* God works for good with those who love him" and that now (but actually only because that signature is valid) it is precisely the empty hands that shall be blessed, because they have long since lost all human hopes and consolations; that the worst sinners shall be comforted, because even the last shreds of any illusions as to their own consequence have been stripped away from them and now for the first time God has a chance to work in them. Now we have the assurance that those who come with nothing in their hands will learn, to their humiliation, that God is *everything* to them. When they hold the hand of God they learn that fabulous certainty with which we can step into the uncertainties of each succeeding day. We have the signed statement, sealed by the sufferings of Christ, that now those who go aimlessly stumbling through life are literally surrounded with joyful surprises, because they will learn (on this *one* condition, that they really dare to trust God) how God is always there, that his help is supplied with an almost incredible punctuality. They learn how he sends some person to help us up again; how he allows us to catch some word (which need not even be in the Bible) to which we cling; how he brings money into the house and bread to our table; and how in the hour of our greatest sorrow he may perhaps send the laughter of a little child.

He who dares to live in this way, in the name of this miracle, in the name of this opened heaven will see the glory of God, the comforting stars of God shining in the darkest valleys of his life and will wait with all the joyful expectancy of a child for the next morning where the Father will be waiting with his surprises.

For God is always positive. He makes all things new. And the lighted windows of the Father's house shine brightest in the far country where all our "blessings" have been lost.

Blessed are you—not because the far country cannot take away from you the dream of home and better times to come. No, blessed are you because the door is really and truly open and the Father's hand is stretched out to you—as long as he who came in the name of the Father stands among us and proclaims, nay, fulfills, the words, "Blessed are you!"

2

The First Installment of Happiness

"Blessed are those who are persecuted for righteousness' sake, for theirs is the kingdom of heaven.
"Blessed are you when men revile you and persecute you and utter all kinds of evil against you falsely on my account. Rejoice and be glad, for your reward is great in heaven, for so men persecuted the prophets who were before you." —*Matthew 5:1o-12*

In every one of us there is no stronger drive than the desire for happiness. It is so strong that as soon as we achieve one happy goal we are immediately on the lookout for new shapes and forms of happiness. No sooner has Faust attained and satisfied his desire than he desires again:

> And so from longing to delight I reel,
> And even in delight I pine for longing.

So happiness is constantly changing its shape and is always just ahead of us. For one it may be money and success, for another the satisfaction of accomplishment, for another the comfort and peace of being at home at one's own hearth. But whatever form it may take, we all pursue it.

And because this is man's deepest desire, everybody who covets power and craves to be idolized and loved by men is eager to emblazon happiness on his banner. They know very well that they will soon be cast into the discard if they fail to promise and produce happiness. People are not satisfied with mere ideas

11

and good intentions; these do not appease this strongest of all urges, this secret yearning for happiness. So the politicians, not by any means only the cold, calculating Machiavellians, but also the most idealistic of statesmen (if they had to begin their careers in times that were dark and hopeless, having only demands to make and nothing to give), have always promised happiness at least for the *future*.

One need only look at the world, running its unswerving course on these age-old tracks, beating its traditional path to happiness, to judge how completely new and totally different are the rules of life to which Jesus subjects us.

I ask you quite simply, does anybody know of a single example in history or has anybody ever heard of anything in the present, that is even remotely like what Jesus says here to his disciples? Have you ever heard of anybody daring to say, "Humanly speaking, I have nothing to offer you but the enmity of the world and the shrieking of demons. I do not give you a seat in the cabinet, but rather deliver you to public scorn. I send you out [just think how ridiculous, how utterly mad this is!] as sheep in the midst of wolves." Have you ever heard of anyone saying this and then not going on to say, "But when you have fought your way through you will reap the fruit of your labors; the world will finally acclaim you and sing your praises, shouting 'You've won, you've won, despite it all!' "?

No, instead Jesus says, "You will never get away from persecution and tribulation; the servant will never be greater than his master, and this will go on until I come again. There may be times of prosperity—and why shouldn't Christianity too become the fashion, all kinds of things have become the latest craze?—and men may shout 'Hosanna' to you. But just wait, just wait a little while, and the cries 'Crucify him' and 'Barabbas' will follow. The Son of Man has nowhere to lay his head and of you too it will be true: here we have no lasting city. This need not necessarily mean you will always be cast out; but believe me, whether it be merely the slightly contemptuous tolerance with which people observe you saying your table prayer in a restaurant, or going to church on a Sunday morning, or whether it be some great political system that challenges your faith, believe me, in every age to the end of time there will be those who will see to it that you are surrounded with an atmosphere of homelessness."

What a ghastly prospect! It makes one ask in all seriousness how Jesus could ever have gained disciples with an appeal like that. And then does it not sound like sheer mockery for him to go on and say, in the face of the tortures of body and soul to which they were actually exposed, "Rejoice and be glad"? If that is not mockery (and surely it cannot be that), then there must be some great mystery here which we do not see.

Did not all of us sense something of this dark, yet gladdening, mystery during the days when the church was being persecuted? What was it that comforted us during those darkest years and, hopefully, will comfort us again when the persecutors begin the chase again? Was it the fatuous, or at least very platitudinous, phrases like "One must not give up hope" or "Lies have short wings" or "Harsh rulers never reign long"? Did the thought of what would happen to our persecutors in the Last Judgment make us feel a little better? Was it not something altogether different that set us on our feet and made us glad again? Was it not rather some word that assured us that in all these things we were only enduring the holy sufferings of our Lord himself and being honored with his fellowship by bearing his cross? And honored in a way that no spiritual exercises or devout worship could ever accomplish? Were not all of us who suffered with Jesus Christ incredibly blessed in a way that we would never have dared to dream was possible and actually never would have been able to discern by way of "theory"? And has not this fact, that cross-bearing is full of hidden blessings, always left the world standing in bewilderment before the spectacle of Christians in Nero's arena or on the scaffold or in the concentration camps, not merely bearing it with set teeth, but singing songs of praise to heaven, not merely lying down and taking it, but lifting up their heads because their redemption was drawing near, because they knew who was coming to meet them on the other side of their torments?

Why, then, did they know this mysterious happiness? For nobody can make us believe that this was merely masochistic pleasure in suffering or a morbid death-wish. After all, they were people just like us; they loved life and the sun as we do; they too had loved ones to leave behind; and their hearts too swelled with flooding joy in anticipation of the coming of spring and the rich beauty of summer. What, then, is the secret of this blessedness in the midst of suffering?

One reason we have already mentioned: that all who suffer for Jesus' sake are given a share in the sufferings of their Lord. Indeed, we may actually set it down as a rule of the kingdom of God that to every man who touches even the fringe of his garment, to whomever suffers even a little reproach for the Savior he gives himself wholly, just as he did for the woman who suffered from an issue of blood. She merely touched him and then he allowed her to perceive the whole of his glory.

All of us would like to "know" Jesus, and we understand very well why the Greeks said, "We would see Jesus." Hence we are inclined to expect a miracle, to wish for a deep, thrilling conversion experience, to perceive the stirrings of the Spirit, as it were with our nerves, hankering after holy feelings. But all this, even if it were bestowed upon us, would pass away again like "sound and foam." But the man who touches him *here*, at the fringe of his reproach, the man who befriends the outcast who is nevertheless the brother of the Savior, the man who cheerfully bears the scoffers' mutterings and lifted eyebrows as he stands up for his faith or risks his all, in fear and trembling and yet with smiling confidence for the sake of his

Lord, that man receives the *whole* of him, in his happy hours *too*. Then he realizes that he is not only standing beneath the Cross but also lying in a grave, and that the imprisoning stone is rolled away from it only because now he is dealing with the Victor and Prince of Life.

There is another comfort, however, in the fact that Jesus promises that his followers must endure sufferings; for the very fact that all this is stated beforehand in his words assures us that suffering is by no means contrary to plan. No matter how grim the fears that surround us, none of it can frustrate the plans of our Lord; on the contrary, they are all exactly in line with his plans. Time after time we learn from experience that it is not the suffering itself that is the worst; the worst is meaninglessness. For the disciples the worst thing about the sufferings of their Lord was not that now they saw themselves facing persecution and torture, but that all the torment of rack and scourge that he would have to suffer suddenly appeared to have become meaningless and worthless. If the Messiah himself ended in bankruptcy, what possible sense could there be in losing even one drop of blood for a lost cause? *That's* why they fled from Golgotha; it was not the threat of suffering; it was the paralyzing threat of meaningless suffering.

Once we see this, the comfort in our text becomes apparent; suffering does not sabotage the plans of God, nor does it contradict the promise of our Lord. Rather he has taken it into his calculations, and it is the profoundest reality in the kingdom of God. Only through suffering can we enter into glory. More than that, only in suffering do we become aware of the glory of God, because it pleases God to have men cry to him out of the depths and to send his only begotten Son into the depths.

But there is something still deeper in this prophecy to the disciples that they would have to suffer. When Jesus foretells suffering, this is far more than a mere prognosis, a mere prediction. In this too Jesus is altogether different from men.

When a physician says to me, "You have only so and so long
to live," he can say this fairly calmly, for his own fate is left
quite untouched. But when Jesus says it, we sense something
different. When he speaks of wars and rumors of wars, when
he foretells the coming of wolves who will break into the sheep-
fold, when he faces us with the danger that love will grow cold
even among the faithful, when his words summon before our
eyes all the woes of the world, from nights of bombing to the
loneliness of those left behind, then all this suffering the world
must endure to the end of time is, as it were, drawn together
in his vision, as space is swept together and focused in a tele-
scope; then he himself suffers this dreadful scene, this terrible
fate, in his own soul. And this, then, is the second comfort:
nothing can happen to us that has not already entered the
Savior's eye and wounded his heart. It was all there in the
Savior's eye and soul long ago and remains there, everlastingly
present in his heart. Do you understand—*everything*, everything of pain and grief that faces us now?

Then, having reached this point, we have also gained access
to what is meant by the words in the Sermon on the Mount:
"Your reward is great in heaven."

At first we may feel a certain hesitation about these words
and perhaps something in us may even react rather vehemently
to them. After all, we know that we must do a thing "for its
own sake" and not be on the lookout for reward.

But the fact remains that no conviction, not even the consistently ethical conviction we have just mentioned, can make
do without the thought of reward. Even the consistently ethical
person knows something of the satisfaction and happiness that
may come from doing a thing for its own sake: "Virtue is her
own reward." So we may twist and turn as we will, but the
idea of reward cannot be eliminated, for the simple reason that
the word "reward" does not mean an outward or inward re-

muneration in material or ideal values, in money or distinctions, but rather because the idea of reward constitutes a kind of scale to express the value of an act and indicate to what extent God can take pleasure in it.*

And here Jesus makes it clear to us that men will dispute every form of this reward that will come to your Christian action, your sacrificing, your prayers, your faith, your witness-bearing. They will not only try to deprive you of all actual *earthly* reward; you will not only fail to see your prestige increased by faith; you will not only come to see that the faithful do not by any means have things better than others (the time of the bombings gave us opportunity to have some realistic experience of that); but often enough you will even see the *inward* reward dissolve into nothingness. Very often you will not even have the reward of peace and joy in believing that you might expect would come after a courageous, straightforward act of witness. Even *this* reward is not something you can count on with certainty. For every Christian comes, sooner or later, to the point where the happy self-evident certainty goes trickling away through his fingers. Cannot the flood of tribulation swell to such proportions, may not injustice so overrun the world, that even the faithful (especially and precisely if they think they are exempt from the onslaughts of wickedness and injustice) are tormented by the question: How can God let such things happen? Can there not and *must* there not be many times when they feel their love grow cold? Even in the midst of persecution for one's faith such temptations constantly recur, though we are inclined to think that the genuine martyrs simply enjoy as a matter of course the reward of inner peace, or to put it less emotionally, the satisfaction of having done a good deed.

We need not have been immured in a concentration camp to have experienced this. We need only to have been exposed

* For further discussion of the idea of reward see chapter 7, "Does Faith Pay Dividends?"

to the cold cynicism of a scoffer or the repeated self-assured shrugs of despisers around us to be pitched into the age-old temptation of believers: Why do the wicked prosper? The complete self-assurance of a definitely godless person, the observation, for example, that our witness does not even provoke him to opposition, but is for him simply airy nothingness (remembering that what *he* thinks is hot air, what *he* thinks he can treat as simply nonexistent is the very thing that our faith declares is determinative of *his* destiny in time and eternity), this is often apt to assail not only our nerves but also our faith and corrode our trust that the "Christian life" is its own sufficient reward. Even for the martyrs, for all who sit behind bars under the ban of the godless, does not the moment come when they are compelled to ask the question that troubled John the Baptist: "Are you he who is to come, or shall we look for another?" the moment when, despite all we know of the Cross, we simply cannot go on believing that *both* are true and *both* continue to exist at the same time: the rule of godlessness in the world, the self-assurance of nonchalance *and* that royal figure to whom all authority in heaven and on earth is given?

But there is still another respect in which reward for so-called good deeds is uncertain and illusory for all who have suffered for Jesus' sake. They are constantly troubled by the thought that they may not have confessed their Lord *aright*, that they may have compromised him, that they might have done it better, that in this *one* case which has brought suffering upon them they might better have kept silent, that it might have been more prudent and wiser in a spiritual sense to have acted differently. This presentiment that what we do is in vain "even in the best of lives," that even in what we do as witnesses and believers there is still so very much that is human, that arrogance, false pathos, the desire to play our little miserable, posturing roles, and perhaps even vain angling for a martyr's crown may lie concealed in what we do—this presentiment never ceased to

trouble the martyrs of Jesus, and doubtless this cannot be otherwise, for they too, and they especially, are the ones in whom
the pious desires of the flesh must be condemned and consumed
by divine judgment.

Provision has been made, or better, God has made provision,
that we should not escape this disquietude, this "human-all-too-
human" skepticism about this reward which a good work is
supposed to "contain within itself."

Note the way it is expressed: "Which it contains within *itself*."
Now we must listen very, very carefully: Jesus says that the
reward of those who suffer for him is great "*in heaven*"; he does
not say that it lies in the work itself.

What does "heaven" mean here? It does not mean that the
work is its own reward (it cannot be, because it is always subject
to doubt) and it does not mean that it will be "repaid" in the
life to come.

"Heaven" is rather the realm, the sphere in which God's rule
is in full and absolute force. Jesus taught us to pray, "Thy will
be done, on earth as it is in heaven," in order to indicate that
even in this world that is loaded with opposition to God, even
in this world where, notoriously, God's will is *not* done but
notoriously opposed, situations may occur in which God's will
is done, fully, completely, and uncompromisingly, just as it is
in heaven.

So, to confess the Lord and to receive reward for it in heaven
means to have a part in this rule of God even here and now,
which is to say that even here on earth by confessing his name
we help in a tremendous way to break down the walls of separation so that God's power can break through to us. Our witness
and confession has a liberating power.

This, then, is our reward—that now, in confessing him, in the
very *act* of confession, we are permitted to learn that we are *not*
strong men who stand up like Luther (actually a misunderstood
Luther) and strongly and passionately declare, "Here I stand,

I cannot do otherwise," and thus as men who are relying on their own strength and courage. Nor does confessing mean that we stand like strong oaks of the Lord with mighty roots clutching the earth as the storms of godlessness, doubt, and mockery sweep through their branches. (What shaking reeds and glimmering wicks, what miserable doubting Thomases we are, even though a few people may have called us confessors and fighters for God! Let us not fool ourselves.)

So, "confessing" does *not* mean that we are like oaks, weathering the storm by our own power. To be a confessor means to bear witness to the power of the living God and to start from the fact (note this, from the *fact*) that this power of God is a force that sovereignly embraces the good and the evil, the faithful and the mockers, and that nothing is beyond its dominion.

But when I do this, when I venture to do this, a *miracle* happens; for then what happens is nothing less than my proceeding to make room for heaven, to break a path for the reign of God in our lives. And just by doing this, my confession gains the power to detonate a greater power; what happens is simply that now I let God act and rule, while I am content to be only his instrument. And when that happens, or better, when I *let* this happen, then I am acting in good earnest with the faith that "our commonwealth is in heaven" and that here we are acting in the name of one whose name is above every name.

You see, then *this* is my undreamed of reward—that in confessing him I am actually set down in this commonwealth, that I release the powers of heaven, and that I myself can retire behind the God who, in my confession, enters the battle and is now the "right man" who will fight for me.

And what a really great reward that is! When I confess God I am not standing in front of him to defend him (as if *I* could protect God!). It's just the other way around; God is standing in front of me and I am standing behind him; he is fighting my cause and I can confidently trust it to him. To confess actually means simply to give the reins into God's hands, knowing that he actually *has* them in his hands already.

This is my reward, this is what it is—suddenly to be a citizen of heaven, the heaven that here breaks through with power and which I, poor, weak man, can serve by being the breach through which it enters, and in whose service I am privileged to be spent and consumed—perhaps in suffering, dying, and in the contempt of men.

Did we not experience this a thousand times in the years of terror and persecution just past? Did we not learn what an incredible, gladdening reward comes to a man once he lets God act on his own, precisely when, from any human point of view, things were utterly hopeless? How often during the worst time of persecution it happened to me, when I simply made the venture—and, of course, many others, who were by no means the least in the kingdom of God, managed to do this in quite different ways—and despite all considerations of prudence and self-preservation, ministerial and ecclesiastical, dared to confess my Lord publicly in situations that were perhaps not un-dangerous, and then was able to say joyfully, almost exultantly: "I'm through, I've made it! Now what comes of it is God's responsibility. Now I have summoned God into the fray. Now I have taken away the initiative from human prudence and opened the way for the action, the sovereign action of God. And this God of mine will not fail where *his* honor is concerned."

Is it not more than sufficient reward to be able to eliminate oneself and taste the blessedness of knowing that God himself rises up to perform his mighty works and that, in the midst of the earth, where the powers clash and the terrible battle rages, I have been transferred into the unspeakable peace and safety of heaven, which is now breaking through and unfurling the banner of the kingdom?

Here we can experience what we must call a real presence of heaven in the midst of our life, in the midst of this aeon, a presence which Jesus elsewhere explained to an astonished audience with the words, "The kingdom of God is in the midst of you" (Luke 17:21). It is already there, wherever he is, for my Lord walks beside me whenever I march against the devil, sin, and death.

But joyful and promising as all this is, it is nevertheless only "first aid"; for the blessedness of this presence of heaven on earth is only a feeble shadow and foretaste of what God will do when he is all in all, when the dark glass is swept away and his own face will shine as the sun, when faith will end and we shall see him in blessed nearness.

The ultimate greatness of this promise of Jesus is that heaven is not only the *goal;* already it shines above our path. It is not only a promise; it is a blessed presence—for *those* at any rate who earnestly rely upon it. And the most earnest form of relying upon it is undoubtedly that in which I confess my Lord and dare to cast on him the whole responsibility for what may happen to me.

Now do we understand why these verses—despite all the dangers of which they speak, despite the daily skirmishes in which we must maintain our faith, despite the great occasions of suffering, which may involve the concentration camp and "goods, fame, child, and wife"—do we understand now why these verses are nevertheless imbued with a surging stream of exultation and why they keep soaring between these two shining poles "Blessed are you" and "Rejoice and be glad"?

We walk beneath an open heaven. What matter then whether our path runs through dark valleys and awful chasms? We know who is watching over us. We know that the terrible deeps, the abysses of life, and our fear of what men can do can no longer swallow us up and that underneath us are the everlasting arms. If we fall, then it is into those arms that we shall fall.

In conclusion it remains only to ask whether all this has not

been untimely and out of date. Has not the church of Jesus
Christ, you may say, withstood these hard temptations about
which we have been speaking, and is it not now enjoying a
respectable, at least fairly respectable, repute?

Hold on, my friends, hold on! Who knows whether this may
not be the stillness before the greatest storm of all? Are we
not already aware of the specters hovering over ancient Europe?
May it not be that today the church must sow unrest and dis-
comfort (simply because it is eternally obligated to speak the
truth in season and out of season, both to our own people and
to others), and that even tomorrow it may reap the storm, which
will once more cast it completely upon *him* who rules the winds
and waves and spreads his open heaven above all the blood and
tears.

We may well pray that the church may not grow soft and
secure in this brief respite in the lee of great events that are
surging all around us. To a hazardous degree the voices of
security are making themselves heard, sometimes even with that
pharisaic undertone that shows no more distress over a people
that was led astray. Here and there we see signs of a kind of
gladness and rejoicing in which God can take no pleasure and
to which the promise of our text certainly does not apply. Let
us be watchful and gird our loins! Storms will come which we
shall not be able to withstand with valor, but only with joy. For
one thing is sure: we are not facing an abyss that is locked and
closed for ever; the beast has yet to arise from it in all its mag-
nitude and inevitably it will come upon us. Once again, we
are not facing closed abysses; but we *can* count upon an opened
heaven and the jubilant chorus of the saints in light whose song
comes forth to meet us: Blessed art thou, my faithful child!

3

The Salt, Not the Honey
of the World

"You are the salt of the earth; but if salt has lost its taste, how shall
its saltness be restored? It is no longer good for anything except to
be thrown out and trodden under foot by men.

"You are the light of the world. A city set on a hill cannot be hid.
Nor do men light a lamp and put it under a bushel, but on a stand,
and it gives light to all in the house. Let your light so shine before
men, that they may see your good works and give glory to your
Father who is in heaven." —*Matthew 5:13-16*

I wonder whether we comprehend the full enormousness of
what Jesus is saying here? After all, what he is saying is this:

"You disciples, standing here before me, you inconspicuous,
insignificant people, you miserable little crowd (far more miserable than you realize yourselves, for I alone can see what you
will do, how you will falter and fail in your little corner, how
you will fall asleep when you should be watching, how you will
deny me when you should confess me), you wretched little troop
—*you are the salt of the earth and the light of the world.*"

Listen carefully: Jesus does not say, "You *should* be the salt
of the earth" (as if we could accomplish this), but rather, "You
are salt and light, simply because your Father in heaven called
you to be salt and light." Do you understand this? For it means
nothing less than this: "The whole earth will be salted and lighted
by you. The world will have to reckon with you. The state,

industry, politics, culture, all will be within the sphere of your power." Isn't that enough to make one wonder if here somebody is not speaking sheer nonsense?

There is a tremendous soaring passion in this saying.

We need to talk about *Christian self-confidence* in order to express this passion. It is true, of course, that he who would boast should boast of his weakness. We know that we are weak and helpless and that it is *God* and he alone who is powerful in the weak; but the fact remains that there he really *is* powerful. In them (and this means in you, in me, and in the whole of poor Christendom) he is so mighty that it produces a great trembling and vibration in the whole body of the world, just as the body of a giant ocean liner is shaken by the pounding of its engines.

The New Testament reveals this trembling to us on every hand.

Unbidden the great scenes in which this trembling and vibrating of the world is perceivable rise before the mind's eye. There is Jesus, the nameless Galilean, appearing before Pilate, the representative of the world's power, and being dismissed with the miserable gesture of Pilate's washing his hands. We can almost hear Pilate saying to himself after bothering almost more than was fitting with the case of this Nazarene, "Next case, please." After all, this was a mere bagatelle for the state to be troubling itself with. And sure enough, the next case did come, and another and another, a whole chain of those who desired to be servants of this Lord and share the lot of their Master. They were dragged before kings and ministers and the highest courts, for the powers of this world always like to be legitimate and legal. They seek to get justice and law on their side when they want to eliminate the nobodies, the people who have neither a name nor a visible lord to back them up and yet dare to speak as authoritatively as if their "imaginary lord" had actually been given all authority in heaven and on earth.

The mighty ones do not rise from their thrones and official seats when the little people come in. Why should they? Should an elephant run from mice, should the directors of the universe and the warders of the machinery of state be upset when a few sectarians talk big? . . . and Pilate said to himself, "Next case, please."

But look, out of this insignificant scene in the governor's office in Jerusalem there went a great trembling throughout the Roman empire, a trembling and quaking laid hold upon the earth and shook the foundations of the world. Suddenly the question of Jesus Christ was spilled out of the saltcellar, and it is almost amusing to see Pontius Pilate, Herod, the Roman emperors, and countless philosophers and poets trying furiously to get it back in again. It had scattered salt in the world and all the scraping and chemical washes could never get it out again. But what Christ set in motion with his few Christians in that first onslaught was only the first precursory sign of the last great crash when everything will sink in ruins to a cosmic grave and God himself will descend upon the rubbled plains of overthrow. Verily, we ought to realize the tremendous claims, the soaring passion of Christian self-confidence.

We find in the New Testament more of the same kind of scenes:

We see the foolishness of the Cross rising up against the wisdom of the Greeks and regarding that wisdom, for all its impressiveness, of which even a man like Paul was well aware, as ultimately nothing more than refuse (I Cor. 1 and 2; Phil. 3:8).

We see the poor in spirit rising above the sick and drunk with power, as the pride of a king's child may exalt itself above slavery and servitude from which it has been exempt through the gift of an incomprehensible and gracious freedom.

Even nature itself, with all the sublime power of its laws and the infinite variety of its forms, groans in travail and yearns for this freedom of the children of God, which these few poor and despised men may call their own (Rom. 8).

Yes, even the light of the sun will fail, the moon will turn

as it were to blood, and the sea will be no more, with a groan
the cosmos will sink into ruin. What tremendous forces and
powers are these! But the little band of those whose love has
not grown cold will be saved, and the catastrophe of a sinking
world will not be permitted to draw them into its vortex, for
they are secure in the peace of the Father.

Only One draws near to the falling world from the other side,
because he is the King. And in his name Christians even now
walk the earth as victors, because they die as those who are
poor and yet rich beyond all measure. *That's how great Christians are!* They belong to the greatest of all kings. True, what
they have is a borrowed greatness, but it *is* greatness. The world
and the lust of it (the whole monstrous world!) will pass away;
but he who does the will of God (and, after all, that's what
this tiny band, almost swallowed up in the world's mess, is trying to do), *will abide forever!* Do you hear that—*only he will
abide!* Everything else will vanish. History will stop, nature
will collapse, the curtain will fall; but he who does the will of
God is more than world history, more than nature, more than
all the peaks of intellect, more than the whole cosmos. *He is more
than all of this*—do you understand? Even though he be one of
the "nobodies," whom the world never notices, yet he dwells
beneath the Father's good pleasure.

Starting, then, with this thought, I believe we may have gained
some understanding of why Jesus made that tremendous statement that we are the salt of the earth and the light of the world
and that the little, wretched band of Christians is nothing less
than the very sustaining power of the world!

Now, what does this mean?

Bernanos in his famous novel, *The Diary of a Country Priest*,
said that it is significant that Jesus did not say, "You are the
honey of the world," but rather, "You are the *salt* of the earth."

To look at many Christians who are soft and effeminate and

sweet one would think that their ambition is to be the honeypot of the world. They sweeten and sugar the bitterness of life with an all too easy conception of a loving God. They soften the harshness of guilt with an appallingly childish romanticism. They have retouched hell out of existence and only heaven is on the horizon. When it comes to the devil and temptation they stick their heads in the sand and they go about with a constant, set smile on their faces, pretending that they have overcome the world. For them the kingdom of God, that comes with the savage agonies and travail of history, the excesses of the Antichrist, and the groans of martyrs, has become an innocuous garden of flowers and their faith a sweet honey they gather from its blossoms. And this is also the reason why the world turns away, sickened and disgusted, from these Christians. People in the world know that life is harder than that, and therefore they know that it is more decent to bear the bitterness of it without sugaring it over.

But Jesus, of course, did not say, "You are the honey of the world." He said, "You are the salt of the earth." Salt bites, and the unadulterated message of the judgment and grace of God has always been a biting thing—so much so that men have revolted against it and even bitten back at it. It has always been easier to get along with the honey-god of natural religion. Where there is salt in a church and in its preaching there is bound to be a sour reaction against it. For salt always bites and stings at the points where we men have wounds, where we are vulnerable. We want healing *without* pain—and besides, we do not even want to be reminded of these sore spots. That's why the world not only shouts for the golden calf but also for the honey-gods who will make us forget our deepest wounds.

So where there is no bitter reaction to the message, the true salt is lacking. It is a dubious sign if the world lives too peacefully with the church. It is not a good sign when people are all too admiring of their preacher, for then as a rule he has not been scattering salt from the pulpit. The people have not been bitten by that preaching; they have gone home thinking they were quite healthy and sound, that they had *no* wounds, and the good Lord has let them get away "with a whole skin." Enthusiasm and excessively unanimous agreement with a sermon usually indicates that it is suffering from a serious deficiency disease.

Then, too, salt has a preserving power, the power to stop decay. Our Western world has become a world of decay and rottenness because that salt is lacking. True, we have made progress, technologically we have reached the heights, we have discovered the delights of life in this world; we love the *joie de vivre* of sunburned young flesh. Ah, but the worm and the canker may be in it. And what a pass we have come to with our ideal of sun-browned affirmation of life, the awful abysses a world without God can plunge into, this world enraptured with its own delights—well, we have experienced it ourselves and with such a vengeance that I need waste no more words over it.

All of us—including every conceivable freethinker, atheist, and antitheist—are still living, far more than we realize, on the Christian heritage, the "salt in the flesh" that keeps it sound. But the organism of our world has gradually used it up. That's why we need Christian disciples who carry salt into the world and help to immunize it against the poison of decay and corruption—against all the processes which have been rather portentously called "the decline of the West."

But there is still another important attribute of both salt and light.

Both become useful only when they give of themselves, when they are mixed with something else and sacrificed. Light goes into darkness and salt loses itself in the dough. How a few grains of salt can change a whole quantity of food or dough! From a purely quantitative point of view, the proportion of really earnest Christians to the whole mass of people in the world is comparable to the few grains of salt in a great mass of dough. And when we Christians grow discouraged; when we think how few we are, of how we stand alone in our family, the place where we work, among our acquaintances; when we are dismayed and fear for our faith at the thought that the kingdom of God which is to triumph over the world is represented by these few insignificant men and women, often enough these few *old* men and women, then we should take comfort from this saying of Jesus. He did not say, "You are the great mass of the world," nor did he say, "You, my Christians, shall be identical with the mass, you will be the citizenry of the world." No, he said, "You are the pinch of salt in the mass," and by its very nature that is a small quantity.

So, do not groan about being a solitary Christian, a small minority in a far greater pagan environment; you have been called to salt this whole godless mass. *That is the promise given to lonely Christians.*

And actually, how often the power of this *one* grain of salt turns out to be mightily effective!

When *one* Christian does not laugh at a particular joke, then that salt seasons the insipid fidelity of the rest.

When this *one* person practices forgiveness in a company that is poisoned by intrigue and enmity, then all of a sudden there is a healing factor in the situation.

When *one* Christian is willing to stand up for his faith where this is hard to do, then suddenly the whole atmosphere of a meeting or group may be salted as with a fresh sea breeze and the earnest spirit may suddenly open ears that were closed before.

When *one* person, in a group that is shaken by fear, thinking of the terrors that may befall the world (which, of course, can happen at any moment), or simply resigning themselves to a hopeless future, when this one person radiates that peace of God which is beyond all the reason and unreason of the world, and thus communicates something of this peace of God to others simply by his presence there—then the salt is doing its work in the midst of corrupting care and paralyzing dread, then the light is shining in the darkness of panic terror.

Once again we say, the solitary Christian is given a great promise: he is a grain of salt. This promise is not given to the whole mass of dough—except as it allows itself to be salted. But this *one* Christian not only has the promise but, since he is a grain of salt, is also the bearer of the promise. And this is his responsibility.

But, of course, if he is to share this promise and fulfill this responsibility, he must get out of the saltcellar. It's so easy, so nice to stay in the saltcellar! This is where the good people are; here they are comfortable together, here they understand one another. That's why it is often so hard to get Christians out into the mass of dough. They would rather let the world go its own way to corruption, and they comfort themselves by saying that it is lost anyhow. They are afraid they will be infected by the children of the world, afraid to soil themselves with politics, afraid their inner life will be injured. But, of course, the truth is just the opposite. He who stays in the saltcellar loses his saltness, not he who goes out into the mass of dough. Why don't we take the promise and command of Jesus seriously? Many people say, "I must grow more strong, I must strengthen my own inner life, before I am ready to speak to others or confess myself a Christian openly. I would rather stay in the saltcellar." You *fool*, don't you know, haven't you heard that the spirit of God will give to you abundantly and tell you what to say, and that you will grow only by getting out of the saltcellar? But you *must* get out, or else you will never find out that this is true. Your inner life grows in doing the tasks your Lord has set for you, but certainly never in the saltcellar.

Most Christians are stupid. That is to say, disobedience is always stupidity (in the full sense in which the godless are called fools), though most people think that it is wisdom and prudence that prompts them to disobedience. I noted, for example, during the church struggle with Hitler, when hard and often dangerous decisions had to be made, that when a person could not summon up the courage to be obedient and blindly trust God's promises he always had the shrewdest arguments and most elaborate tactical reasons for making his disobedient, and in the long run stupid, compromises. So it is in this case; the Christian remains in the saltcellar because he thinks that here he will be best preserved. He wants to be wise, he wants to be sharp— and in the very act loses his saltness. Salt works, salt remains salt only as it gives of itself.

Or a Christian puts his light under a bushel simply because he is afraid that the winds that blow in the evil world, among his friends in the factory or office or school, who do not believe, will blow out the light of his faith. The fool! If he would only dare take Jesus' promise seriously and simply leap joyfully into life wherever he lives it, he would see that the light will not be blown out by the wind, but actually rekindled, and that God, who has given his promise, will never let the glimmering candle go out. But when that candle is kept under a bushel its light helps nobody, and, what is more, it exhausts the oxygen and nothing is left but a nasty, guttery wick.

When the kingdom of God breaks in on the Last Day, God will first destroy the saltcellars and overturn the bushels; for the judgment of God will begin with the household of God. And I fear that then Christendom will present a very sad picture, a conglomeration of tasteless salt and evil-smelling wicks. And saddest of all will be that the very ones who were most religious, the very people who heard the Word of God together and knew *more* about the promises of God will constitute the largest contingent of this rubbish.

So, there you have it, a biting, salty truth that will sting in some pious people's wounds. But I could not withhold it from you and myself. And it is to be hoped that no one will think it is *the others* who are meant.

Salt and light live and work by sacrificing and giving of themselves and *not* by trying to "preserve" themselves. In any case, Jesus Christ, the faithful Salt and the loyal Light, did not choose to shine in the glory of heaven and to preserve and save himself in the pleasant climate of the kingdom of God. No, he came as a light in the darkness of the world, right down into the midst of reeling, staggering, unhappy humanity. And if we are all still alive and the world is given a reprieve, and if this brief reprieve is not a last respite until we are all blown to bits by the madness of the atom bomb, but rather a reprieve of grace, then it will be solely because the *one man* did not remain in the heavenly saltcellar (if you will pardon the expression!) and hide himself under the divine bushel, but came down into our world and gave himself all the way from Bethlehem to Calvary. It is actually blasphemy to think that heaven is a saltcellar and a bushel. But do not we Christians act as if it were? And when we do so, are we not denying our Lord and denying the deepest intent of his sacrifice?

So salt and light have one thing in common: they give and expend themselves—and thus are the opposite of any and every kind of self-centered religiosity. Salt works and expends itself in secret, and you cannot see it operating. One thinks of the quiet, unobtrusive influence of a Christian upon his environment, his family, his associates, which he exerts just by being what he is, by being there in prayer and in love. One also thinks of what the New Testament is referring to when it speaks of those who, "though they do not obey the word, may be *won without a word* by the behavior of their wives" (I Pet. 3:1).

Light, on the other hand, can be seen; it works openly and visibly. And here one thinks of the church's task of witnessing publicly to the gospel and of sending men and women into all branches of public life, in politics, industry, culture, and above all, education. God gave his only begotten Son for this world; therefore we must be light and salt for the world. And certainly the world is worth serving by our sacrifice. Why? Simply because this *one man* poured out his blood for it, because this *one man* first sacrificed himself for us all.

You must be the little grain of salt for the little bit of earth that God has entrusted to you. *You* must be the glimmer of light for the little world where you live and have your being.

4

The Costs of Grace

"Think not that I have come to abolish the law and the prophets; I have come not to abolish them but to fulfill them. For truly, I say to you, till heaven and earth pass away, not an iota, not a dot, will pass away from the law until all is accomplished. Whoever then relaxes one of the least of these commandments and teaches men so, shall be called least in the kingdom of heaven; but he who does them and teaches them shall be called great in the kingdom of heaven. For I tell you, unless your righteousness exceeds that of the scribes and Pharisees, you will never enter the kingdom of heaven.

"You have heard that it was said to the men of old, 'You shall not kill; and whoever kills shall be liable to judgment.' But I say to you that every one who is angry with his brother shall be liable to judgment; whoever insults his brother shall be liable to the council, and whoever says, 'You fool!' shall be liable to the hell of fire. So if you are offering your gift at the altar, and there remember that your brother has something against you, leave your gift there before the altar and go; first be reconciled to your brother, and then come and offer your gift. Make friends quickly with your accuser, while you are going out with him to court, lest your accuser hand you over to the judge, and the judge to the guard, and you be put in prison; truly, I say to you, you will never get out till you have paid the last penny.

"You have heard that it was said, 'You shall not commit adultery.' But I say to you that everyone who looks at a woman lustfully has already committed adultery with her in his heart. If your right eye causes you to sin, pluck it out and throw it away; it is better that you lose one of your members than that your whole body be thrown into hell. And if your right hand causes you to sin, cut it off and throw it away; it is better that you lose one of your members than that your whole body go into hell.

"It was also said, 'Whoever divorces his wife, let him give her a certificate of divorce.' But I say to you that every one who divorces his wife, except on the ground of unchastity, makes her an adulteress; and whoever marries a divorced woman commits adultery."

—Matthew 5:17-32

Probably all of us still remember what was drummed into our ears some years past: "Faith in God is something for the weak, the craven, the losers. We steer by our own power; we run on our own steam."

In the face of such an assertion, are we not reminded that this faith broke down and overthrew the strongest of men? Did it not hurl Paul trembling to the ground before Damascus? And was not Luther, instead of being provided with crutches and illusions, nearly burned to ashes under the consuming gaze of the majesty of God, only to rise from this fearful collapse and go forth a new man?

Every man who would go to this Father must first pass through the most dreadful of danger zones. Every man must face the eyes of the Judge. Every man must face this question, a question which is utterly intolerable without Christ: What do I look like in the light of the law of God; and, if I must see myself so (even for a moment!), what do I look like in God's eyes?

Anybody who would become a new man must first die. And in this text it is Jesus, this Jesus who brings us to peace, or better, who himself would *be* our peace, who sets us down in the midst of the consuming flame of God's majesty. He sets us down at the point where we are at the end of our tether. If there is anybody who hopes that in Christ the real danger spots of life are rendered harmless, that nothing else can ever happen to us, because, after all, he is the "kind Savior" who takes back even hardened sinners with no questions asked—well, that person must first come to terms with this text, which says that this Jesus Christ does not subtract one jot or tittle from the severity of God's will, that he came not to abolish this threatening law, but rather to fulfill it, indeed, to make its profoundest threat apparent. The truth is that grace is not cheap, but tremendously costly. What could be more costly than that for which a man must pay with his life? And Jesus demands nothing less than that, if we want peace: we must die, utterly, radically, and un-compromisingly. Without death there is no peace, but only fear, or failing this, only the narcotization of fear that the worldling seeks.

Not long ago on a lecture trip a taxi driver drove me some distance across country. I should like to recount some of our conversation because I want young people especially to under-stand as clearly as possible what I mean by "costly" grace.

My companion said, "I have heard that you are a theologian." I said that this was so, and he went on to say, "I'm not a Chris-tian, you know; I really believe in paganism. But you needn't get out of the car, for I too believe in higher powers."

Whereupon I turned around and asked him, "Where, then, do you have your mascot doll hanging?"

"No," he replied, "I don't have one in the cab, but I do have a moneybag over there in the glove compartment. That's my talisman. But what makes you bring that up? We were talking about something else."

"Oh," I said, disregarding his mild reproach, "I can tell you a lot more than that. You don't like to drive on Fridays and furthermore, you're quite miserable if you have to start out on the thirteenth. You are also interested in astrology, and I would be willing to bet that more than once you've had your horoscope cast."

He looked at me in such amazement that we almost drove into the ditch, despite the talisman.

"How do you know all that? It's true."

"It's because I know my neopagans well," I replied. "These people are very uneasy in a world without God; that's why they need all this stuff. 'Wise' people like you always have a touch of persecution mania. You are always seeing the world full of trees, all waiting to ram into your radiator. One might also say that you have no peace; that's why you resort to talismans and incantations and try to figure out your fortune by means of a horoscope."

"Well now, that's putting it a bit too strong, what you say. But you're not altogether wrong. Anyway, you said something about 'peace.' That's what we want. . . ."

Here I interrupted him and said, "And surely you know, I hope, that you will never find it in this way?"

"Oh," he said, "I feel quite satisfied about it. This little jigger," he said, pointing to the magic moneybag, "has really worked pretty well. But you mustn't think that I despise the church. I tried Christianity once too, just because it says something about *peace*."

"Well," I said, "you really did put your finger on the best and most important thing in it. That's pretty rare for non-Christians to do. May I ask what it was that stopped you?"

"Shucks, I might as well tell you; it was simply because I can't take this stuff about *Christ*. I don't understand how anybody can believe in a God-man. How do you know all this stuff the Bible says is true? For those who can believe it, O.K.; I don't bother with them. But as far as I am concerned, I can't believe it."

"And *that's* where your peace broke down?" I asked. He replied, somewhat embarrassed, "Well, yes, naturally that's what it was. But anyhow I already told you I don't feel so bad at all."

"Let me tell you straight, will you, what is the matter with you," I continued. "In the first place, you don't feel well about it at all, but, like an old campaigner and taxi driver, you naturally won't admit it. And, believe me, you won't get anywhere on

THE COSTS OF GRACE

the road you're going. What you're trying to get is an all too
cheap peace. All this stuff you do costs you nothing. You are
probably a good bargainer and you're figuring pretty closely
in this business too. You want to get as much as possible for
the lowest possible price. First you want inner composure, what
we just called 'peace.' But more than that, you want eternity
and you want to get by the Last Judgment. Or are you going
to say that all these dodges, your talisman, your astrology, your
respect for Friday and the thirteenth of the month, are going
to pass you through unscathed and get you off very cheaply?
After all, you can go on living with these things without
changing at all! And this little bit of brooding and thinking
you do about whether there is anything in Jesus Christ, when
you're waiting for a fare and have a little time on your hands,
this naturally will *never* solve the question for you. The Lord
Christ has never yet held out any promise to those who merely
do a little brooding and thinking about these things."

"Hold on, professor," the man beside me retorted, "after all,
I can't buy a pig in a poke. I can't turn my life inside out and
pay a big price for someone I don't even know, somebody I
don't even know ever lived."

"Nevertheless," I said, and said it as plainly and unrelentingly
as possible, "that's just what you have to do. Christ said that
only he who wills to do the will of the Father in heaven will
know whether his teaching is from God. Understand, only he
who *does* the will, who is in *earnest* about it, who *stakes* his life
on it. God is known only by those who venture, just as all great
things in life are seen only when we are obedient and downright serious about them and not when we look at them from
the easy chair of speculation and noncommittal curiosity. And
something more: don't think you will get by with a little philosophy like 'do right and fear no man.' Your talisman doesn't
trouble you at this point at all; it's far from exercising even a
bit of moral control over you. But with Christ the first thing

you will be shown is that never in a thousand years will you be able to stand up before God. At first Christ is always very disturbing. You are dealing with the God who leads men into hell and out again. You are a nice, easygoing worldling (you don't mind my saying this straight out?) and you have settled down comfortably in your world-view. You are really convinced that you have not settled down in hell. But if you are in earnest with Christ, you will have to give up your comfort and peace of mind, not because you are supposed to become a nervous worrier, but because it is a false, delusive peace, which you keep propping up with the power of suggestion and your little magic devices. But God loves the brokenhearted and the poor in spirit who have no illusions about their own wretchedness as they stand before the face of God. As long as you have not met God as one who opposes you, you haven't met him at all. Don't you see that this is something different from all the magical cribs and crutches and rickety footbridges that you are trying to use in order to cross the chasms of life? You have already gained a great deal in at least coming to the point where you realize that these things you are walking and standing on are only tottering makeshifts and that beneath you lies an abyss."

Our conversation went on for a long time and even though, when we came to the Neckar River, he did not, like the Ethiopian eunuch, say, "See, here is water! What is to prevent my being baptized?" (Acts 8:36), I was nevertheless grateful that in this brief hour together something of the peace of God and the hopeless desolation of his world had been communicated to him.

The thing in this conversation which seems to me to be important for the understanding of our text is this: that at the very beginning and as a kind of introduction to discipleship, Christ makes us feel the implacable severity of the law and thus leads us to death.

We should really stop to think what this must have meant to those who were listening to him. After all, they were within a tradition in which God was taken with an immense seriousness. Every step was related to God and taken as it were under the eyes of God. From this there had developed a system of legal prescriptions that kept a person constantly on tenterhooks and never allowed him to be certain whether he had *really* measured up to the will of God. All of us know pretty well what this amounted to among the Pharisees. But we need nevertheless to guard ourselves against ridiculing this earnestness and being too quick to dismiss it as "morbid legalism." Perhaps it really was a rather morbid form of taking God seriously; just as today, when we meet a hard, legalistic Christian we sense a certain morbidity and the effect it has on us is always somewhat chilling and repulsive. But is it any less morbid not to take God seriously at all, any less pathological than calling upon him only at marriages, funerals, and a few times when we are in a tight spot—and even then for the most part only as a matter of form?

In any case, we need to understand what it meant to these people, that into this world, with its fine-meshed network of laws, in which one felt more a slave than a child and where there was no chance of anything but getting more hopelessly entangled in the snares of guilt and accusing conscience—that into this world there came One in whom one sensed the nearness and immediate presence of God and found it to be nothing less than fatherly, saving *love*. What a wonderful thing it was that here should come One who treated a man like a brother and brought him back to the Father's house! How incredible and liberating that he should simply take one by the hand, even if one's hands were soiled! This really was something different from the servile drudgery of serving the law, in which a man was never sure whether he had done enough and, as we would say today, never wholly got over his inferiority feelings.

But here is this very One who seemed to be able to liberate a man and let him breathe again saying: not one jot shall be removed from the harshness of the law. Indeed, more than that:

he made this law so radical that the people's eyes filled with
tears and many of them would have preferred to turn back,
saying: "Even with Moses we had it easier; there at least we
knew where we stood. And even if we never quite fulfilled
the commandments, the disparity between our lives and what
God demanded was at least tolerable and, above all, we could
see what it was. But this Jesus of Nazareth demands the *whole*
of us, and even declares that the innermost, secret thoughts of
the heart belong to God. He casts us all into utter hopelessness,
and, instead of mitigating the demand, he increases it. Or is it
possible that he means something else when he says, 'Unless
your righteousness exceeds that of the scribes and Pharisees, you
will never enter the kingdom of heaven' "?

This faces us with two crucial questions about this text.
First, why is it that Jesus proclaims the will of God to us so
radically, so utterly demandingly (or should I say "crushingly")?
And *second*, how can we cope with it?

To begin with the first question: Jesus makes it clear to us
that God's demand lays claim not only upon our *acts* but even
the thoughts of our hearts.

Naturally, we are not all murderers and adulterers in the outward sense. In this respect most of us have fairly clean hands.
But what about our hearts? Do we not all have in us what
Adalbert Stifter called a "tiger-like tendency" which is so hidden in normal life that one might think it wasn't there at all?
Do we really know "what unknown beasts may not be evoked
within us by the dreadful force of the facts? All the forces that
suddenly emerge when life situations occur in which the usual
inhibitions are gone? For many of us was not the prison camp,
with its hunger pains, its lust for life, and its extreme nervous
strain, such a place where that "dreadful force of the facts"
was released, a place in which we were shocked at ourselves and
the beast in others? Those others who hitherto had been decent
or at least passable comrades? Did not many, even of the young-

est, acquire a knowing eye, because for a moment or for several weeks or months they were forced to look at a mere *fragment* of what God's eye sees in us day and night, hour after hour, far behind and deep beneath our outward acts?

The point is that God sees deeper than our normal, foolish eyes that merely linger on the surface of things. He sees the many thoughts that are on the ready for murder and adultery. He sees the consuming jealousy that is eating us as we shake hands with our competitor outwardly and secretly wish he were in Jericho. He sees the impure glances and the furious eagerness of our imagination. And when we go a step deeper, into the witches' cauldron of the unconscious, from which our life is so largely controlled and in which are brewed the dreams that horrify us, the picture looks even more sinister. The psychiatrists can tell us something about this. But, we ask, does not all this— the thoughts of the heart, the unconscious mind, our dreams— constitute an area that isn't really a part of "me," because, after all, "I" am only the conscious mind, the part that understands and controls? Or must I not say: this too is "*I*." These are *my* thoughts, this is *my* imagination, this is *my* murdering and lying and adultery, even though these things never see the light of day.

Why is it that they so seldom see the light of day?

Perhaps because I haven't the nerve, perhaps because I have too many inhibitions that are tied up with my position in society to do too openly what I have the urge to do. I have an interest in wanting to be respected by people, I am afraid of the *consequences*.

Perhaps, perhaps I also do not murder and lie and commit adultery because it is clearly forbidden by God's law and because I have respect for his commandments. But at the very moment when I feel the command of God as an inhibition and allow it to restrain me I perceive why it was that I was restrained. The commandment of God makes me all the more conscious of the opposition, the rebellion that is within me and the terrible

hostility of the parties that are warring within my soul. (Anybody who wants to see what that means has only to read the
seventh chapter of the Epistle to the Romans.) I may be fighting
a fierce battle with sin and for a moment I may think that I am
fighting something alien to myself. But *I myself* am the antagonist.
It is not the "sin which dwells within me," but *I myself*. Paul
knew all about this (Rom. 7:20).

That's why the law must remain in all its severity! It must
remain like gauze in the deep wound in our heart, to keep it
from healing too easily and forming an invisible scar that would
fool us into thinking that we are not wounded and sick at all,
that we do not need anybody to die for us and to forgive and
heal us as a savior.

Are not all of us in danger of removing this gauze and not
only deluding ourselves with some smooth kind of healing but
even imagining that we were never really so badly wounded
and sick after all?

We all know what the *Christian education* of youth has meant
for our whole nation. But it is no disparagement of this positive
contribution of Christian instruction to point out that there is
also a danger in it. From our youth up we have been taught
to take it almost for granted that God is prepared to forgive
everything and that the seal of our baptism has been stamped
upon this full pardon. We have in our pocket a document in
black and white to prove it. Why, it was there in our cradle
and now, as licensed possessors of a baptismal certificate and
contributors to the church, we can produce it any time we
please. Even Peter will have to let us in when we pull our
"pass to heaven" out of our pocket. And certainly there will
be at least standing room for us in heaven.

That, you see, is the other side of the medal. On one side
is stamped the great and genuine seal of mercy, but on this side
—well, I think you understand what I mean.

There is a danger of being sure of forgiveness before one

has become insecure because of one's sins. It is possible to come out in the end with the view of Heinrich Heine who said, "God will pardon me, it is his trade," thinking we can be quite assured that at the right moment God will do his duty to our satisfaction:

> Always happy, always happy,
> Every day is happy day,
> For the Father up in heaven
> Calls us his little children.

Rather soppy and infantile, isn't it, even though it is most certainly true that God calls us his children. But because we are his children, blood was shed, and that's something that is absolutely *not* to be taken for granted; for this the Cross was raised on Golgotha, for this the very heart of God was wounded. How then should we forget our own wounds!

But if we do forget, then we take grace for granted. And that's the worst. Then you can have it cheap, dirt cheap—like some half-decayed merchandise thrown in for anybody who will take the stuff away with them. Then this grace becomes merely another term for the innocuousness of God. The Last Judgment becomes a monstrosity of perverted medieval imagina· tion and the law of God is transformed from an electrically charged barbed wire that separates us from the majesty of God into a hedge of roses in whose shadow one can booze and carnalize and murder and play the black market to one's heart's content. And therefore, in order that *that* should not happen, Jesus here breaks open our deepest wound and stuffs it with gauze, however severely it may hurt. Suddenly the Crucified is facing us here; and before we hear his cheering, redeeming words, "This have I done for you," *we* must daily be heard saying, "This have I done against thee." *Only then* will we comprehend the cross of Calvary. Otherwise it becomes so innocuous that ladies dare to use it to ornament an evening dress.

It should be clear by now that here we are dealing with a terribly serious matter. It is so serious that Luther said one must necessarily go down to despair and utter ruin because of it. And we all know how he himself was shattered.

But this brings us to our second question, the despairing question: How can we ever get across this terrible chasm that separates us from God, this chasm that is no less terrifying for all our expenditure of energy, wit, and spiritual training in seeking to blink and evade it?

Luther once said that "at first" God is my accuser and my heart my defender. What he meant was that when God addresses to me the whole, unconditional law that makes its absolute claim upon me, as is done in the Sermon on the Mount, my heart immediately moves over to a defensive position and says to me: "How can God demand this of me? You really cannot help it if evil thoughts spring up in your heart and all kinds of things bubble up in your unconscious mind. You are responsible only for that sector of your ego which you can control as an acting, willing, conscious person. You can say," whispers my conscience, arguing as my attorney, "that any demand that goes beyond this sector is not your responsibility."

But then comes the second act, says Luther, and the tables are turned. Here my *heart* is the accuser and *God* is my defender. What Luther means is that in the second act, when God has overcome me, my conscience can only say to me in all candor: "You did *not* come from the hands of God in the state you are in now, with all your ulterior motives and all the evil impulses above and below the threshold of your consciousness. Therefore everything that is in you is charged to *your* account." But then God makes the ultimate reply to this self-accusation; he tells me that *he* will take over my defense and that he will not allow these terrible things that are in and behind my thoughts and words and deeds to separate me from him.

Look, that is really all there is to it: to let God defend you,

or better, to let Jesus Christ take up your cause! But in letting
him take up my cause, I never lose the consciousness that there
is something within me *against* which he must fight. In letting
God defend me, I know that there is something within me
against which he must defend me. And that preserves me from
pride and carelessness.

What a tremendous, almost incomprehensible thing this is!

What God does is to take me into protective custody against
myself, by setting me down beneath the Cross. Now nothing
can harm me, now, above all, I cannot harm myself.

There is my *accusing conscience;* never am I safe from it.
How it loves to keep gnawing constantly or suddenly to spring
upon me in the middle of the night, confronting me with the
secrets of my heart. But then within me my divine defender
cries out: *"Christ is here!"* I am in his care and custody.

There is *death*, that keeps lying and telling me that all life is
meaningless, that all will sink into nothingness. But then comes
the voice: *Christ is here!* If I live, I live in him, and if I die, I
can only die to *him*. Whether I live or whether I die, I am with
him and nowhere else.

There is *suffering*, grinning, unmeaning, unmanning suffering,
the misery of the whole earth and all that rocks me in my own
life. And here again comes the voice saying, *Christ is here!*
Everything that strikes me must first pass before him, and all
the horrors of history cannot finally prevent it from reaching
the eternal goal of his love and ending at the foot of his throne.

Because God reaches out to me with his love, because he
suffered for me, because his heart beats for me as he comes to
meet me on the steps of the Father's house—*that's why*, and that's
the only reason why I can love him in return. That's the only
reason that, suddenly, I am able to fulfill the whole law. For,
after all, love *is* the fulfillment of the law. And here we see a
great mystery becoming clear. We begin to see why the law

can never bring us to the goal, why it can only wound us and keep us wounded.

For I cannot love by being commanded to love. Commands only restrain me. But to obey, to rein in and stop always means that I have to overcome, fight down something within myself. It is the base man, the old Adam within me that is subject to commands, the old Adam of weariness, of fear, of defiance. So when I merely obey commands I am never there as a whole person, but perhaps at most only with the better half of my self, while the other half remains in opposition. But when I love I am there as a *whole* person, for love is a movement of my *whole* heart; love is always an overflowing, limitless giving of one's self. Therefore it can never be commanded; it can only happen.

In other words, I can only give my whole heart when another whole heart gives itself to me. I can only love if love is shown to me.

And this is precisely the miracle that occurs when I stand before Jesus Christ. For there I see the Father's heart, the heart that tore itself away from that which it most loved, the only begotten Son; the heart that bled for my sake; the heart that beats for a man who stands in the lowest place and dares not even to lift his eyes. And this man is *I*.

Look, now I can love the One who suddenly stands beside me in the lowest place, instead of remaining in the glory of heaven.

What the thunders of Mount Sinai could not accomplish— the liberating of my heart to make it free to love, to be a child, and to feel at home in the Father's house—this is accomplished by the one who comes to me as my brother.

Coming down to the depths to fetch me, he says to the Father, "Look, here I bring him; I have bought him at great price." And because and on account of my brother, Jesus Christ, I *can* come.

So now when we hear the words, "We love, because he first loved us," we know that this is not a "command" or a "law." We know that this answering love is only an echo that wells up overwhelmingly in my heart, an echo of an exultant certainty: I am loved, I am loved, I can come to God!

5

Every Word an Oath

"Again you have heard that it was said to the men of old, 'You shall
not swear falsely, but shall perform to the Lord what you have
sworn.' But I say to you, Do not swear at all, either by heaven, for
it is the throne of God, or by the earth, for it is his footstool, or by
Jerusalem, for it is the city of the great King. And do not swear
by your head, for you cannot make one hair white or black. Let
what you say be simply 'Yes' or 'No'; anything more than this comes
from evil."   —*Matthew 5:33-37*

This text* speaks of the sacredness of our word. It says that
every "Yes" and every "No" we utter is spoken absolutely and
before God, and that every word, including many a wave of
the hand or gesture or wry face (for these can say far more than
words; they can speak volumes!), that every word of ours is
deemed so important that the Last Judgment will concern itself
with them and will surprise us with a precise enumeration of
every careless word we have uttered (Matt. 12:36).

But how can we account for the fact that what we say has
such weight? Can we take this at all seriously?

Just think of all the driveling words that are spoken, written,
affirmed in lovers' oaths and never kept, hissed in hatred and
later rued. Think of the words that fly from mouth to mouth
on the gray wings of rumor, all quite anonymous and nobody

* The chapter heading is the formulation of Julius Schniewind.

responsible. Think of the thousands of "Heil Hitlers" that have thickened the air, and the thousands who disassociated themselves from it all with the lame excuse that it was a word without content, an empty matter of form. The question is, however, whether the Last Judgment will take the same view. And here we are told that all these words are stored away in eternity and that they possess an infinite weight and consequence. Can one really take words so terribly solemnly, so frighteningly seriously?

Here is Faust, sitting in his study, opening his Bible. He is irked by the opening sentences of the Gospel of John: "In the beginning was the Word."

> Here now I'm balked! Who'll put me in accord?
> It is impossible, the *Word* so high to prize,
> I must translate it otherwise.

And finally, as you know, Faust decided to say: "In the beginning was the *Deed*."

Now I suspect that I am speaking for all of us when I say that all of us, moved by natural enthusiasm or perhaps by a fierce grief over the terrible declension of man's speech and writing, might wish to take this dictum, "It is impossible, the *Word* so high to prize," and make it our own.

And yet, if we as Christians have strong inhibitions about accepting this Faustian translation of John's Gospel, and thus subjecting even the *divine* Word to this universal depreciation of speech and words, then undoubtedly the reason is that there really is no difference between what the Gospel of John calls the "Word" and what we in our language call "deed." *When God speaks, this is no empty talk: then something happens; when he speaks it stands forth, it is done* (Ps. 33:9). This world of ours was created through the Word, and therefore this Word of creation was an act, a deed. And when Jesus Christ says to a sick and guilt-ridden man, "Rise, take up your bed and walk," and he actually rises, takes up his bed and walks, then we realize how charged with action this Word is, that it is always an active, operative Word and not merely the descriptive, theoretical speech of a teacher. When Jesus Christ speaks, something always happens to upset and change things. Then this Word takes hold of my destiny, looses or binds me, brings healing or curse—and it does this simply because it compels me to decide. No man can go on living as he did before once this Word has plunged into his life. The truth is, this Word *is* a deed.

And precisely the same thing, namely, that words are deeds and not merely empty talk, is true of the words of *men:* "The tongue is a little member and boasts of great things. How great a forest is set ablaze by a small fire!" (Jas. 3:5). Was not the whole forest of the world, that stood in flames for five years and still goes on dangerously crackling and crepitating, set ablaze by *words?* By words that concluded treaties and other words that broke the treaties; by words that counseled aggression; by cunning words that inculcated ideologies and legalized even the most atrocious deeds; by words that called evil what was good and called holy what God has forbidden? Do not words cause and move and sustain our whole history? Who could even conceive of the millions of graves and the ruins—if there were no words? Do not blessing and joy prevail where a good word is spoken? And back of family strife, back of hatred and spite are there not always words, venomous, coiling, writhing, serpentine, death-dealing words? Is there any one of us who does not know a word that definitely helped him and perhaps gave him peace and who does not know other words that still stick like smarting thorns in his soul?

Ever since the Word became flesh and thereby determined every human destiny, ever since man has had to take a stand with respect to that event, ever since he has had to accept or reject that act and, accepting or rejecting it, go on to the Last Judgment, where again he will have to give an account of himself in *words*—verily, ever since then, words and speech are no longer mere sound and vapor; now they are freighted with eternity, charged with destiny and responsibility that determines life and death, containing the sparks not merely to kindle forest fires, but the very fire of eternity itself.

The gates of hell are opened by *words* and by *words* they are closed. Blessing and curse, salvation and condemnation are inclosed in words as in gracious and yet mysterious vessels.

This, then, is the background against which these words of Jesus concerning swearing and the seriousness of our words are spoken in the Sermon on the Mount. Here is ground we can tread upon only in fear and trembling. We can enter it only with a knowledge of our own lostness, only as we cry out in awe and confession: Lord, I am a man of unclean lips.

If we could believe many expositors of the Bible, we could, of course, quite cheerfully skip this passage altogether. (Has anybody preached on this text at all in the last twenty years?) For we are reassured that naturally this prohibition of swearing has nothing to do with our judicial oaths and any serious pledging of our word of honor. And the sigh of relief that escapes us when we hear this consolation becomes even deeper when we are assured at the same time that the Lord himself employed oathlike formulations. But, we ask ourselves, is swearing really such an innocuous thing? Or ought we not to start by taking very seriously the fact that, according to Jesus' statement, sin does not manifest itself only when perjury is committed, but even in taking the oath itself and therefore in certain solemn forms in which I speak the truth and nothing but the truth?

Let us look at this closely and ask ourselves what actually happens when I swear an oath. When I utter the form of oath, "I swear by God. . . ," inherent in this utterance is the following:

In the first place my oath always has the character of being *exceptional*. That is to say, I do not always swear, but rather I solemnly disassociate by means of an oath a particular statement from my ordinary, everyday speech. I invoke the name of God "exceptionally" in making an affirmation. But by the very exceptional way in which I do this I am really saying: *ordinarily* God is not necessarily present in what I say, and therefore my ordinary speech does not have the same degree of bindingness and earnestness which I now want to emphasize. In other words, I am trying with the help of an oath to increase artificially the specific gravity of my word, and by this very token I am admitting that ordinarily my word does *not* necessarily possess this specific gravity, and hence that "as a rule" I merely float along on the stream of ordinary chatter.

Once you discover this fact you will recognize it in all forms of asseveration. What do we mean, for example, when we say, "I give you my word of honor"? Surely we mean: I vouch for it, I stake my reputation upon it, I will stand or fall by what I say. But the very fact that I must emphasize this explicitly means that "as a rule" I am not present in my word as in a home, but rather let my tongue run around freely like a tramp.

Let us say I have told my child the old story of the stork, because his question made me uncomfortable. I merely indulged in a bit of stupid talk. And, I say to myself, I can permit myself this kind of irresponsible talk, because, after all, everybody does it. The child, I tell myself, will sooner or later find out what the true facts are. (But do I consider that by planting this harmless untruth I am at the same time sowing a very small seed of distrust in this child's heart, which perhaps will not spring up until the time of puberty, when my child avoids me as far as these questions are concerned?) But what if, after the telling of this silly stork story, the child should suddenly ask—and certainly this is something he *never* does!— "On your word of honor, father, is it really true? Are you willing to stand or fall by this story?" Then we would sud-

denly realize that our word had no specific gravity at all and
that once more it was nothing but empty talk.

Or if I said, "I have no time," or if I said any number of
times, "Heil Hitler," and somebody asked me, "On your word
of honor, do you stand or fall on that?"—I would suddenly
realize with horror that I had been babbling irresponsible stupid-
ities, that I have been playing the hypocrite and lying, rep-
rehensibly and carelessly playing with the bombshell of human
speech which is loaded with all the powers of heaven and hell.

And is not all this really horrible, utterly terrifying? Whenever I utter the formula "I swear by God," I am really saying,
"Now I'm going to mark off an area of absolute truth and put
walls around it to cut it off from the muddy floods of untruth-
fulness and irresponsibility that ordinarily overruns my speech."
In fact, I am saying even more than this. I am saying that people are expecting me to lie from the start. And just because
they are counting on my lying I have to bring up these big guns
of oaths and words of honor in order to drive a breach into
these abysmally pessimistic prejudices of my fellow men, this
closed phalanx of distrust (and quite *justified* distrust too!).

A sign of increasing deceit and a correspondingly increasing
mutual distrust in our day is the almost inflationary increase
of oaths and loyalty pledges. How many oaths were demanded
during the Third Reich, from Hitler Youth cubs to pensioners;
how many questionnaires we had to sign and solemnly swear
to in the presence of witnesses and guarantors, because words
had become cheap, because they had lost their eternal weight,
and men had to look around for something artificial to use as
makeweight. We pray that our people, who have been literally
educated to hypocrisy (and are still being so trained in the
East!), a hypocrisy in which almost every word meant something different from its ordinary signification (nor was the
church by any means a hundred percent exception!), have not
lost the Word for ever. We pray that they may still find their

way back to the *real* and *true* Word and in that Word regain the trust of others in the veracity of what they say, so that, having this *one* Word, all their other, everyday words will be given weight and bindingness. May it be given to them to find this *one* Word, without which all others are as shifting sand, and that is: "My Lord and my God."

He who has learned to speak this word, this word that *responds* to *God's* Word, becomes uniquely credible in a world of deceit, because he knows the face of God and has begun to speak in his presence.

In his controversies with the Pharisees, Jesus calls our attention to another subtle form of lying: "Woe to you, blind guides, who say, 'If any one swears by the temple, it is nothing; but if any one swears by the gold of the temple, he is bound by his oath' " (Matt. 23:16).

Back of this saying, which sounds rather involved and remote from our own way of thinking, there is a message that goes directly to the center of our life today.

In the oath that is quoted the Pharisees evidently meant that when a man swore by the temple one could not hold him to it absolutely, even though what he said might be true. But when a man swore by the *gold* of the temple, then there could be no quibbling and twisting, then he must stand by his word.

In other words, by general agreement there are cases in which one does not have to speak the truth, cases in which there may be a mental reservation.

Once we put it this way we immediately sense that it directly concerns us.

For among us too there is this tacit, openly secret understanding that certain things we say are not binding. Certain forms of courtesy give occasion to affirm the opposite of what one really thinks. Then there is the big subject of *white lies*, including everything from saying "I don't have time" to telling

the maid to say that "Mr. and Mrs. are not at home," while they
are sitting comfortably at tea not ten steps away. In the army—
but certainly not confined to it—there is a well-developed technique for not telling the truth about certain things, a vocabulary
tested by centuries of usage that indicates what one is to say
in this or that situation and what one conceals while saying it.

In any case, there are in the life of human society certain
areas in which by universal agreement what we say is not taken
seriously, in which our word has almost completely lost its
specific gravity. Consequently, a person who was accused of
telling a lie when he said that he was not at home to a visitor
would actually feel that he was being unfairly slandered, since,
after all, a little white lie like that is beyond good and evil,
because it is, so to speak, sanctioned by society and one must
not weigh every word so scrupulously. I am afraid, however,
that the combined weight of all the words we have not carefully weighed here below will quickly tip the balance in the
Last Judgment. Hermann Bezzel, the great preacher, quite
rightly said, "White lies are silken threads that bind us to the
Enemy, invisible webs that are woven in hell."

True, they are "silken threads" which are not seen at first.
In hell everything begins with little innocuous things. The
history of the world began with an insignificant grab for an
apple. In ordinary speech one would never think of calling it
stealing, but probably only "rigging" or "cutting corners," and
yet Cain's murder of his brother, the building of the tower of
Babel, wars and rumors of wars are all related to these little
manipulations. A *murder* begins with the slender, silken fibers
of a few thoughts, quite internal, naturally, and well concealed
in the precincts of the heart where thoughts have their privileged
freedom and nobody can be forbidden to think. An *adultery*
begins with a glance. And the bonds of the greatest passions
were once but silken threads. Just as that which at first hardly
moves the balance finally tips the scales in the Last Judgment,

so the delicate web of trivialities becomes a closely woven net of ropes in which the Accuser seeks to catch us and bring us as spoils to the Last Judgment.

But, you ask, isn't all this a little, or even a great deal, exaggerated and isn't there some good sense in leaving open a few areas of life where we do not need to be so serious about God, where we can play about a bit? Why should this mean that we are really being bound to the Enemy with silken threads?

And this confronts us with a great Christian mystery. The fact is that there is no area whatsoever, which, the very moment it is removed from God—not necessarily with wicked intent, but merely in the sense of declaring it to be a religious no man's land, an area beyond good and evil—is not immediately taken over by the Enemy. And here again the invasion does not begin with beating drums and flying colors; at first it is by no means demonstrative; first he works through his "fifth column," which operates anonymously and in the dark.

But isn't it true that what we here ask for on a small scale, namely, this zone where we can be free from God, has actually become a large-scale reality in our world? Have not men demanded the autonomy of politics, economics, science, and art, areas that have their own laws and in which the law of God has nothing to say?

How small has become the segment of life in which we are still willing to grant supremacy to the sovereignty of God! And when we do concede it, it is at most a kind of limited and constitutional monarchy, in which we men desire to sit in parliament and thus occupy the real key position of power. How dreadfully far we have departed from the earnestness of those words of the New Testament which tell us that *all* power in heaven and on earth has been given to Christ the Lord, and that therefore there is *no* private recess of the heart, no public area of life, no treaty between nations, no word whispered in the dark which is not subject to all his commandments and which will not have to be accounted for in the Last Judgment!

This little study of the gravity of our word really has brought us face to face with the ultimate question. There is One who never stops asking us questions.

And now we may make this simple, practical observation: once a man breaks through this area of little untruths, of conventional lies and white lies and is honest in the sight of God and the Last Judgment he experiences at least two things.

First, he learns how hard it is at first to break through this unspoken agreement on the part of the world. One actually feels a bit queer about it, and at first one exposes oneself to the suspicion of being eccentric.

But then, secondly, we discover what a tremendous liberation it brings when we decide nevertheless to do so—as soon as we have gotten past the suspicion that we are merely being crudely frank and those around begin to see under whose *command* we are. The avoidance of one small fib, which may be fully recognized as legitimate, may be a stronger confession of faith than a whole "Christian philosophy" championed in lengthy, forceful discussions. When I stand before a *superior* in this defenseless, honest openness, renouncing any pretense whatsoever—which means standing before him in the name of Jesus Christ—he will suddenly see in me the representative of my Lord, acting in His name, and all the moralistic self-confidence with which he usually reacts in such cases will collapse. A *subordinate* will see my honest exposure of myself—if I do it in the name of Jesus— not as a loss of authority, but rather as the strength that I can freely afford to show as a servant of a strong Lord.

I will begin to learn that under the dominion of this Lord trust and confidence grow in a way totally different from the way in which I try to gain and keep it with my little fibs and pretenses. I will begin to note in those around me something of that longing for freedom from dishonesty which everybody has within him and which makes him look with eagerness to the Christians around him to see whether this kind of honesty and this freedom of the children of God is really possible in this world and whether it is really true that he whom the Son makes free is really and truly free (John 8:36). Only the man who under Jesus Christ gains the freedom to be truthful—simply because he believes the promise that all who let him be their Lord will not be put to shame—begins to realize what servitude he was living in when he was chained to hell with the silken threads of conventional deceit and mendacity.

Surely we shall not pretend that all this is so much harder than simply submitting to the law of inertia and continuing to lie! In reality nothing is more onerous and afflicting than to be bound to hell; and nothing is easier than to risk the leap into the freedom which the Son of God has promised us and sealed with his death. Here it is really true that "his commandments are not burdensome," for they do not demand that we go out and do battle with a whole world of lies—that could frighten us!—but only that we love him who has already overcome this world of lies. But when this happens it has already been provided for that we shall be made a part of our Lord's overcoming of the world and that we may participate in this overcoming in the victory of Jesus Christ.

What a difference it would make if our "Yes" and our "No" really acquired this significance of overcoming the world, if in every moment they were uttered as in the presence of God, if we were no longer dependent on the expedients of little lies and duplicities, and all this simply because Jesus *has* overcome this world, because we really do not *need* to act as if we must run with the pack, as if there were areas in which he is *not* Lord!

Therefore when we are obliged to swear oaths or give our word of honor in this fallen world we shall always remember that this is only a temporal necessity in a world shot through with lies and that it is only with the help of this expediency

that at least one area in this world is marked off in which by
way of exception the truth is to be told. We should reflect
that this is the same kind of emergency measure or concession
as that of divorce, which likewise may become necessary in an
adulterous world and be allowed by God in his condescending
patience. Therefore with the freedom that we have to say a
simple "Yes" and "No" we should show how gladly we bid
farewell to this world of lies and how glorious is the freedom
of the children of God, who have come into the truth because
they belong to the Lord of truth.

Ever since Jesus Christ became the Word made flesh and thus
honored our human speech by framing the message of life in
human words these words of ours have become hallowed things.
Ever since the Savior hung upon the Cross we feel a certain
repugnance to the use of it as an ornament and frivolous bauble.
But just as the Savior hung upon the Cross, so he also hung
upon words: he was crucified by the words of men, by your
words and mine, the words in which, together with Pilate, we
refused to believe that there is a King of truth in a world where
selfish interests precede truth. He was crucified by words
uttered by you and me in which we solemnly declared that we
want nothing to do with this man who is the witness of our
deepest dishonor and whose pity knows no limits (Nietzsche).
He was hanged upon the word of God's promise that he would
seek us through pain and pay the price for us.

Ever since that happened our human words have been
freighted with the heavy burden of the crucified Savior. So
whenever we demean our human speech to the level of stupid
drivel and deceit and thus empty it of any weight, we are
doing nothing less than throwing off from our words this precious burden of the Savior and consigning him to a second
death, which *this time* will bring us no blessing.

Let us remember, then, this costly weight and gravity of
human words and remember, too, that the same words we use

in our everyday speech are the elements with which our prayers are made. Think of what that means! It means that the wicked thoughts of our wicked hearts may be lifted up in prayer to God, and our tongue, that dreadful firebrand, is able to put these thoughts into words and send them up to God. This is the great transformation of our speech, and it is given to those who live under the King of truth and have begun to taste the royal freedom that he alone imparts.

"Let what you say be simply 'Yes' or 'No'; anything more than this comes from evil."

Say "Yes" to Jesus Christ, and you gain eternity.

Say "No," and you throw it all away.

Two words encompass our eternal destiny.

These two words should also give to our speech in the *world* the character of conciseness and responsibility. But above them all stands the petition: Forgive us our trespasses!

6

No Retaliation!

"You have heard that it was said, 'An eye for an eye and a tooth for a tooth.' But I say to you, Do not resist one who is evil. But if any one strikes you on the right cheek, turn to him the other also; and if any one would sue you and take your coat, let him have your cloak as well; and if any one forces you to go one mile, go with him two miles. Give to him who begs from you, and do not refuse him who would borrow from you.

"You have heard that it was said, 'You shall love your neighbor and hate your enemy.' But I say to you, Love your enemies and pray for those who persecute you, so that you may be sons of your Father who is in heaven; for he makes his sun rise on the evil and on the good, and sends rain on the just and on the unjust. For if you love those who love you, what reward have you? Do not even the Gentiles do the same? You, therefore, must be perfect, as your heavenly Father is perfect."   —*Matthew 5:38-48*

Whenever we hear this, perhaps the most difficult and darkest passage in the New Testament, we are overtaken by two feelings.

On the one hand we feel that we are being taken clean out of this world—the world of distrust, the world of brutal struggle around the feeding trough, the strained atmosphere of a land crowded with too many people, where a multitude of people, each with their own instinct for self-preservation, are competing with one another—and set down in a peaceful countryside. And here there seems to be no suffering and no crying, here the sun of God's mercy shines on the evil and on the good.

"Sweet peace come, ah come to my heart" we feel like saying as we catch a glimpse of this landscape, and there steals over us a haunting sense of what God *really* intends this unhappy, self-devouring world of ours to be.

But then almost at once there comes disenchantment. Is not this country where love rules and enmity is dethroned just a fairyland, an unreal dream? And is it not a painful sign of weakness to dwell on such dreams of a peaceful world with no hate or rancor in it? After all, we have to live this life, this dangerous life as it really is; we have to keep our feet on this earth, even if it is a cruel earth.

Did not Jesus Christ himself endure this earth? Was not his cruel cross rammed down into this very earth—a sign that he knew and was close to its torment and its hardness? So how could we ever seriously suppose that this Jesus—this Jesus who knew better than anyone "what is in man," who cast himself upon the mercy of this beast which is man, in full consciousness of what he was doing—how could we seriously believe, I ask, that this Jesus indulged in visionary daydreams, unreal and alien to this world? At best the beast in man can be caged, perhaps tamed and trained a bit, but it can by no means be ignored or banished. Why should we think that Jesus of Nazareth should be the one person of all men not to have seen this?

No, we shall not be able to dismiss these words that easily. This plausible explanation might perhaps be possible if these words had been spoken by some visionary pacifist who had not yet learned what human nature is. But with Jesus, who knows more about men than anyone else, this is certainly ruled out.

In any case, we must face these words of Jesus with all their problematical difficulty. Besides, I do not believe that it is Jesus' wish that we simply accept everything he says, as it were, "right off the bat." Indeed, the very ones he loved were those for whom faith came hard; simply because they took him more seriously than those who would swallow anything so long as it was religious. The doubters are always more blessed than the mere fellow travelers in faith. For they are the only ones who fully learn that their Lord is stronger than any doubt and any hell of despair.

So let us take our doubt to Jesus and ask him quite frankly: "Jesus of Nazareth, what would happen if we took seriously what you say about turning the other cheek to one who strikes us? What would happen if we did not assert our rights when some slick crook takes our coat and we let him take even our shirt in the name of God? What would it lead to, Jesus, if we tried to love our enemy? Wouldn't that be utterly unrealistic? Wouldn't it ultimately mean being unfaithful to our commitment, which we may possibly have to maintain despite all opposition and opponents? Would not this lead to a characterless obliteration of all the distinctions which you yourself, Jesus of Nazareth, took seriously when you said that you had not come to bring peace, but a sword?

"More than this, the whole order of law would be destroyed by what you say. Would not obedience to your strange commandments lead to anarchy and bloody revolution? Would not the whole underworld raise its brazen face and run loose because nobody would be allowed to oppose it, and would not that result, not in a peaceful countryside, but a dictatorship of scoundrels? Would not this mean the triumph of all the base and brutal instincts? Do you mean to say, Jesus of Nazareth, that this is what you want?"

The fact is that we cannot simply swallow these doubts; and besides—as far as I can see—they arise not only from our own nature but from Jesus himself.

But what would happen if we were to turn the question the other way around?

Assume for a moment that Jesus' demand that we love our

enemies were actually in force as a law. Assume that we were really required by law to be limitlessly and unconditionally merciful. Suppose that this were actually so, and simply because God is limitlessly and unconditionally merciful to *us* (Luke 6:36), because he disregards our enmity and our rebellion—I ask you, then would not the fact that we absolutely *cannot* fulfill this command of Jesus and the fact that this world actually refuses any such fulfillment of it be a sign of how lost and estranged from God this world order is? So perhaps we have no right at all to cast doubt upon this love-commandment of Jesus in the name of the brutal laws of this world and ridicule it as unrealistic and alien to this world. Perhaps we shall have to turn around completely and in the name of this love-commandment call the *world* in question, concluding that it is a world sold out of sin and enmity, a mad, deranged, disordered world. Have not all of us asked ourselves at one time or another—perhaps as businessmen confronted with a host of restrictive regulations and tax laws, or people caught in the mechanisms of general competition and then having to run with the pack, play the game, and go along with various shady, dubious practices if they are not to go under—have not all of us asked ourselves whether it is even remotely possible to carry out the will of God in this world without compromising, even if we personally were determined to do so? And if, in spite of this, we tried to do so, wouldn't we really lose out and go under, just *because* the rules in this world are more brutal than those in the Sermon on the Mount, just *because* you have to *fight* your way through enmities, competition, and opposition, just *because* you cannot *bridge* them over with love—at least if we set any value on keeping at least one foot on the ground and not be left holding the bag every time?

So we must catch very clearly this *one* note in our text. In this text there is an *indictment* of our whole world, a tremendous protest in which Jesus strictly refuses to go along with the conventions of this world, absolutely refuses to recognize the law that one must run with the pack. In it is the note of Jesus' great sorrow over what has become of his Father's world, over the fact that the mark of mercy has been so completely erased from its midst, even though the world itself continues to exist only by this mercy and patience of God. Behind these words of Jesus is the knowledge that God and this world are at cross purposes, that the two live in dreadful contradiction to each other—in a contradiction whose witness is the bloody cross of Calvary.

This becomes especially clear when we consider that here Jesus' mercy is at odds, not merely with certain degenerate aspects of the world, but even with the completely legal and recognized juridical ordinances of our world. For it is true, isn't it, that "an eye for an eye and a tooth for a tooth" is a recognized principle of law? After all, the whole system of civil, penal, and international law in our world is based on counterbalance of values and reparation. How could the world ever be kept in order and balance except through retribution and reparation? *Everything* in life must be paid for, *including* guilt; and therefore the dictum stands: "an eye for an eye and a tooth for a tooth."

And here Jesus seems to be challenging and contradicting this whole process, this whole order of the world. He seems to be setting his face against it in protest.

What is he, a utopian, a revolutionary, to dare to do such a thing? Is he a visionary, a fanatic, who in the end will be crushed under the wheels of this world's order, which, *despite* all his warnings, he could not reverse or stop?

And was it not a hideous irony that this Jesus Christ, the Son of God should actually have been condemned in a legal trial and, apparently, was not a victim of an illegal judicial murder?*

* Many exegetes interpret the trial of Jesus otherwise.

Does not this express all the futility and also the complete dubiousness of this protest?

But I believe that by taking all our doubts as seriously as we have and stating them frankly to Jesus we have already gone too far and gotten off on a wrong path.

Did Jesus really want to abolish all law? In any case our Lord's own conduct throughout his life speaks *against* this imputation.

He by no means simply presented the other cheek to those who struck him, but rather took to task the police who were arresting him (Mark 14:48; John 18:23). Another time, it is true, he suffered in silence and when he was reviled, he did not revile in return (Mark 15:19). He also directed his disciples not to expose themselves defenselessly to assassins on their lonely missionary journeys, but rather to take with them a sword (Luke 22:36).

And did he not also allow divorce at least because of hardness of heart and grant that anyone who was married to an adulterer might separate from this his partner and thus dissolve the marriage on his part—thus answering one solution with another—"an eye for an eye and a tooth for a tooth"? Need I go on and point out that Paul too appealed to Roman law and hence appealed to and went along with the order of this world (Acts 16:17 ff.; 22:25 ff.; 25:10 ff.)?

So the matter is not so simple that we can say that here Jesus was bluntly liquidating all law and order with one mighty principle and that he was the one person in this world who did not see that then chaos and anarchy, but heaven knows not the kingdom of God, would triumph.

In this stark, slashing, striking, and therefore unescapable way of stating it, Jesus is saying to us that human law and justice are incapable of regulating our relation to our neighbor as God wants it to be, but that the law is only a *regulation of necessity* which is necessary in our fallen world.

And here we must become completely practical, so practical that you and I will know that we are being addressed.

Let us think, for example, of the house regulations in an apartment or tenement house. In these days the kitchen and other rooms may even have to be shared with the other occupants and recently arrived refugees. This means that everything has to be regulated even more strictly by means of house rules, in other words, by means of "law."

Nobody can doubt that these rules are necessary, for otherwise the result would be a hopeless, slovenly mess, and in no time at all the decent housewife would be imposed upon by the sloppy ones, having to clean up the mess they have left. This is why there have to be precise rules governing everything from keeping the stairways clean to the use of the laundry.

Now, when I think only in "legal" terms (which in itself is altogether correct), I am interested in the occupant of the floor below or the fellow user of the kitchen only from the point of view whether he is a good, helpful neighbor, a troublemaker, or a sloven.

Then this also affects *my* attitude toward him. If he irritates me by his tardiness, if he upsets all my plans for getting the laundry done, or if he neglects to keep the steps clean, then I do the same thing to him, so that he may get a lesson in what this does to a person. I say to myself quite rightly (and on the *human* level nobody can object to it in principle, though this bit of revenge also gives one a "human-all-too-human" satisfaction): I had better teach him the rule "What you do not want others to do to you, do not do to others."

On the other hand, if he is neat and helpful, he gets a corresponding response from me. The fact is that all life in this world is built upon this law of response in the good and in the evil.

Unquestionably, this is the way things are on the *human* level. But the moment I see the other person *before* God, where I myself stand as a disciple of Jesus, then I know that Jesus Christ died for this other person, this unpleasant, irritating, disagreeable, and perhaps unprincipled person, and by that very act this other person acquires his infinite importance. Before, I saw him only from the point of view of whether he helped or harmed *me*. And so I *myself* was always in the center of all the rules according to which I dealt with him. In the last analysis I was the end for which he was a suitable or unsuitable means.

But now, beneath the eyes of Jesus, the whole question changes. There I no longer stand in the center, but rather the *other person*. There I must ask myself: What has happened that this other person has *become* what suddenly he now is? He may perhaps be a refugee, with a future so leaden and hopeless that he hardly pays any attention to the impression he is making upon others. Perhaps his life has been shadowed by severe suffering which has made him bitter or broken his character. Perhaps too he has an unfortunate heredity and to be quite fair with him one must see him against the background of his whole family. Perhaps too he had a bad bringing up. So I look at him with the eyes of compassion and begin to understand him, because I *love* him as the poor and needy brother of Jesus Christ. Quietly and mysteriously, therefore, my whole standard of judgment has shifted. Now of first importance is that I care about the other person *himself*, that I take him seriously and consider him important enough to dignify him in this way, and that I stop asking what his relationship to *me* is and thus stop taking only myself seriously. In other words, that I stop thinking of myself as the only end which the other person must serve.

Then, because under the eyes of Jesus I see this other person in a wholly new way, with a dignity of his own, the dignity of being a brother of Jesus Christ, I am now compelled to ask myself another question: What will serve his eternal salvation?

What can *I* do, what *must* I do, in order that Jesus may not have died for him in vain? And once I am compelled to stand firm and face that question, then the following consideration will be borne in upon me: If I merely react to him legalistically, if I merely do to him what he has done to me (and nobody could blame me for this!), then I merely harden him, then he will only be driven deeper into his resentment, his bitterness, his cynicism, his slovenliness. And that means that I would be doing wrong to him. I would become the guilty one. When Jesus Christ asks me about him at the Last Judgment, I may perhaps wish to say, "But I acted correctly; everybody told me that I was justified in doing what I did; I did nothing that he did not do to me first." But I shall never get the words past my lips, for suddenly I shall see the nailprints in the hands of the Crucified.

Just because I am no longer merely a "natural man," but rather a man standing beneath the eyes of Jesus, I am suddenly reminded that Jesus *too* did not confine himself to what is correct in his attitude toward me. If he had done so, if he had dealt with me according to the rule of "an eye for an eye and a tooth for a tooth," I would surely be headed for hell. No, I am reminded on the contrary that he called me his brother and shed his blood, even though I was his enemy. But when I remember that, then there is nothing left for me to do but take the lowest way and have pity, just as a mother pities her wayward child. Then I do this, not from weakness or cowardice, but letting the other person feel that I am saying something like this: "What I care about is *you*. Look, my friend, I don't want you to go on running the wrong way. I don't want you to be struggling with all kinds of complexes and embitterments. I am responsible for you before God, and *that's* why, and that's the *only* reason why, I do not strike back, even though I have the right to do so. That's why, and that's the only reason why, I offer you the other cheek.'"

We understand, then, what this strange saying of Jesus means.

To "turn the other cheek" means this: "Look, by taking the lowest way, I am for a moment making myself completely defenseless as far as you are concerned. I am exposing my flank to you, standing here without protection and without weapons, exposed to your possible jeers and your saying that I did not dare to hit back, that I flunked, whereas in fact I was acting in the royal courtesy of *love* and offering you a chance to find yourself and peace again."

And right here I should like to put this question to everybody who has understood what we have said so far: Will not this attitude, will not this royal courtesy of love mysteriously alter my actions also in those cases in which I must not give in, but rather stand on my rights and resist the other person, as may be the case where the cause itself or educational reasons demand it? For parents with respect to their disobedient children and superiors with respect to uncorrect subordinates will by no means always be doing a service to them by taking the lowest way of submission. But even here, as everywhere else in life, it is the tone that makes the music, and it makes a great difference whether a father chastens his son in anger, which means punishing him out of egotism and for the purpose of working off his own anger and getting a certain satisfaction from it, or whether he takes upon himself this painful procedure (and above all, painful to himself) in the knowledge that in this case severity and uncompromising resistance can only serve the other person and are indispensable to his inner welfare and progress. In these cases too, where resistance and severity are called for, a different tone will prevail when a disciple of Jesus acts, the tone that says: "Listen, my concern is for *you*, not that I am only insisting upon *my* rights. It is your soul that will be injured, my son, my friend, my employee, if I let you get away with this. That's why I am resisting you to your face."

A disciple of Jesus who lives under the eye of his Master always acts completely differently from all other men, no matter whether he breaks through the legal conventions in compassion and offers the other cheek or whether he stands on his rights for the other person's sake (and not as a fanatic insisting on the letter of the law or an egotist acting within legal limits). Jesus is not offering us here some new legal prescriptions for our conduct—there could be no worse misunderstanding than this. He is rather setting before us the ultimate *goal* of our action toward others, namely, the reconciliation of the other person, who has been dearly purchased, for whom he poured out his blood.

Our Lord shows us this other person as he stands beneath the Cross. And seeing him there, the disciple *knows*, quite simply knows, that ultimately what counts is not the assertion of his personal rights, but rather that he help this other person, in order that this cross may not have been raised above his life in vain.

May it not be that, confronted with this compassion and this new tone, the other person too will be shaken into a new awareness and that he too will be disarmed, that the letter I have put into his hand instead of insisting on my rights will become a first sign that there is a message, a law in this world that is totally different from what he ever thought possible before—namely, the message of God's mercy that has brought me home and is now coming to him too as he stands beneath the cross of Jesus? In the Gospel of Luke we are told that after Jesus' last dying cry the people beat their breasts in a gesture of remorse. Do you think that would have been possible if beforehand Jesus had not *prayed* for his enemies? This prayer and his love poured down from the Cross had left them disarmed and defenseless and brought them to a new way. Had Jesus accused them from the Cross or threatened them with the Last Judgment (and how right he would have been to do so!), they would only have been hardened, merely fortified in their passionate conviction that they were in the right.

May it not be? Well, it certainly may, and perhaps some of us have had some very concrete experience of it, seeing a neighbor, a colleague, a subordinate, whom we have shown this kind of defenseless compassion, turn around and take a look at himself, asking himself, "What makes him think and act this way? Did he at some time have the same royal compassion shown to him which he is now showing to me? Did he discover that all the hateful, mean, poisonous things that assail him were also within his own self? Did he realize his own pitiful lostness, and is this what it is that causes him to deal with me in this complete lack of pride and to put himself so completely on the same level with me?"

So we help by putting ourselves under the mercy of God and then letting it radiate to others in order that this unhappy world may be disinfected. What can it not mean for a family, a class in school, a neighborhood, a marriage, if there is one single person in it who practices mercy because he himself has obtained mercy!

But now we must ask one last question and perhaps the hardest one: How can I get to the place where I become like that? After all, we don't want to fall victim to pious words that are too beautiful to be true. We have no wish to become addicts of an unrealistic romanticism. The loveliest truths become lies if they cannot be practiced, if one is not "in" and "of" this truth (John 18:37).

So, how can I bring myself to love my enemy?

Well, we begin by asking another question first: How did Jesus come to love his enemies? What actually happened when Jesus practiced that deepest of all love that made it possible for him to pray for his enemies even on the Cross? What he said was: "for they know not what they do." And surely he could say this only if he saw in them something completely different from a sadistic, excited mob of people, a wild crowd of human beasts. He could say this only if he saw in all who stood slavering and shouting around his cross—lost and strayed children of God.

His gaze penetrated the outer dirty surface and saw beneath it something entirely different, something these people were *really* meant to be, that God *really* intended them to be, the plan he had for them. Every person is ultimately a thought of God; true, a dreadfully distorted and almost unrecognizable one, but nevertheless a thought of God. And when the church of Jesus Christ sends its pastors into the cells of even the worst criminals and malefactors and in the night before their execution, in the moment before the law demands its retribution, invites them to the royal table of the Lord, then there occurs the same event that took place in Jesus' prayer for his tormentors and persecutors. Then the church of Jesus bears witness that it still sees in the criminal this thought of God, declares that he is a child of God, recognizes a sonship which he has lost, but therefore once possessed, and now offers it to him again in the name of the sufferings and death of his Savior.

Ralf Luther once expressed it this way: "To love one's enemy does not mean to love the mire in which the pearl lies, but to love the pearl that lies in the mire." So love for one's enemy is not based on an act of will, a kind of "self-control" by which I try to suppress all feelings of hatred (this would lead only to complexes and false and forced actions), but rather upon a *gift*, a gift of *grace* that gives me new eyes, so that with these new eyes I can see something divine in others.

But, you say, isn't this, too, just a beautiful theory? Can this new way of seeing the other person become reality, say in the midst of war or in the hostility of a broken marriage?

Well, I heard once of a woman—she was a Christian—whose husband was really a beastly monster. From any human point of view she could only despise him in his animal sensuality and his sodden, brutal drunkenness. But then, she said, whenever some hateful incident occurred, perhaps when he was facing her with glassy, drunken eyes, perhaps lifting his hand to strike her, and all the revulsion and anger of a violated, betrayed human being leaped up like a flame within her, then suddenly she remembered some nice thing he had said to her in the days of their engagement. And, suddenly, she realized that in this one good word, forgotten, oh, so long ago, the *real* man in her husband was speaking. That one good word was a hint, a glimpse of what God really intended him to be. There, in that word, lay something of the gleam of a pearl now covered with mud.

And from that moment on she could never see in his eyes anything but a deep and hungry cry for liberation and could never look at him without seeing his depraved soul enclosed in a horrible prison, from which he could not escape and in which he suffered a nameless suffering. Suddenly she realized: this monster of a husband is not merely a beast; he is a horribly lost and pitiful child who needs pity and compassion.

Don't you see? This one word remembered from days of love opened it all up and now all of a sudden she saw her husband in an altogether different light. She had caught a glimpse of what Christ saw as he looked down from the Cross.

When this gift of new eyes is given, as it was to this woman, then a miracle happens. When the people who were looked upon with the eyes of Jesus, who realized that those eyes recognized in them their lost and buried sonship, they were suddenly changed and then were able to recover. The eyes of Jesus and the eyes of a disciple not only see the pearl but also "release" it, help to *bring out* the sonship of God in the other person.

And every one of us can have the same experience, if we would. What an indescribable liberation it is for a fallen, hate-filled, embittered, evil person to meet a person whose eyes do not stop at his sordid exterior, and thus merely force him to make his armor of mire and spite thicker and more impenetrable and cover himself with another isolating layer of defiance and stubbornness! What a liberation for him to meet someone who sees through that armor into those dimensions where the publicans and the harlots are still children, beloved and mourned of God!

Believe me, every one of those unhappy, bitter, and wicked people you know are all waiting for this look from the eyes of a disciple, which will better them and heal them—just as you yourself are waiting for it too. They are all yearning for the new eyes, which only *Jesus* can create.

A few years ago I had the experience of meeting the "prodigal son" of a family I visited. He had brought shame and sorrow upon his mother and broken her heart. I was utterly amazed to come in and find him sitting at the piano playing the chorale, "Out of the depths I cry to thee," and playing it with obvious sincerity. And as I was wondering how this could ever happen, I overheard his sister hiss contemptuously, "The rotten hypocrite." I cannot remember now whether she actually said it aloud, but at any rate it was written all over her face. What she was doing was reacting hostilely to this enemy in the family, and, humanly speaking, nobody could say she was wrong. For he really did appear to be a hypocrite, putting on an act.

But in a moment like that must not the eyes of a disciple see something else and something different? Was this young man at the piano really dissembling when he played "sacred music," pouring out in music the cry of a lost child for release and redemption, while he was still in reality a hard-boiled sinner? Or was not perhaps just the opposite true, that in reality he was the child yearning and hungering for redemption, that in reality his fallen state was merely a mask, a dissembling, a distortion of his true being?

Anybody who enters into fellowship with Jesus must undergo a transvaluation of values. The new eyes simply make him see everything differently, but not only that, for these eyes of his also acquire a *transforming* power. As disciples of Jesus, we can, we are permitted, to accomplish the same miracles that Jesus' own eyes accomplished when he looked upon his fellow men who had gone clean off the track, the thieves, the harlots, and the sinners, and saw them as the children of God, and by seeing them so, changed and transformed them.

We should thank God that as the church of Jesus Christ we are permitted to be a company of people who know a better way to treat men than simply to slap down the enviers and haters and opponents, a better way than merely keeping our distance from base, unlovely, unlovable people and associating only with those we like and from whom we get something in return. In this world of hatred and jealousy, of denouncers and scoundrels, of profit-seeking and cold self-interest we need to keep looking for this lost sonship. In this world we Christians have had our eyes opened to see that all who make life hard for us and all who give us a sour reaction are dearly bought and paid for by Jesus Christ. Now our new eyes see Jesus Christ standing among them, eating with them, undergoing the same baptism, and even in the last painful hour of his life refusing to reject them but keeping them close to the tree of the Cross by his prayer and his love.

This Jesus, who stands over there among our enviers and haters, is asking that we take our stand with him and discover the terribly ravaged sonship within our brothers and sisters and with love woo it from its grave.

Don't you see? *This* is the gospel—with all its difficult and strange talk of loving one's enemies. That's what it is. This world which is choking and dying of hate and revenge is *waiting* for the new and renewing eyes of disciples. It is waiting for the eyes that see man's sonship to God and *therefore* also see the bridge that leads to the neighbor's heart and even to the enemy's heart.

That neighbor of yours who gets on your nerves—he is waiting for that look. That fellow worker with whom you are at odds, that son of yours who is breaking your heart and whom you hardly know what to do with, that husband who has changed so sadly and disappointed you so bitterly, and all the others who bring tension and discord into your life. All of them are waiting for you to discover in them what Jesus saw in them and what gave him the strength to die for them. All of them, friends and enemies, the good and the bad, are beloved, straying, erring children of the Father in heaven who is seeking them in pain and agony.

Who else will ever see this child of God in them and lovingly draw it out of them if not you—you who are yourself standing beneath the eyes of Jesus and being seen as such a child?

"As we have received mercy, we do not lose heart" (II Cor. 4:1).

To lose heart, to grow weary and impatient is the worst.

We all too easily lose heart in this life of ours where that sonship to God is masked in so many different ways that we hardly see it at all. But sonship is something that needs to be believed, because the Father of his children must also be believed.

But he to whom God's grace is new every morning will always be fresh, and his love in turn will refresh both friend and foe.

7

Does Faith Pay Dividends?

"Beware of practicing your piety before men in order to be seen by them; for then you will have no reward from your Father who is in heaven.

"Thus, when you give alms, sound no trumpet before you, as the hypocrites do in the synagogues and in the streets, that they may be praised by men. Truly, I say to you, they have their reward. But when you give alms, do not let your left hand know what your right hand is doing, so that your alms may be in secret; and your Father who sees in secret will reward you."   —*Matthew 6:1-4*

During the last week I received a number of letters from people who are standing, as it were, *outside* the door of the church. Their religious opinions were widely divergent, but, quite remarkably, there was *one* phrase that recurred almost word for word in their letters: "I accept the Christian ethic fully and completely."

"The Christian ethic"—this obviously meant something like this: "I share with the so-called Christians a certain way of thinking, a certain way of acting, a certain attitude toward my fellow men. I too am for loving one's neighbor, for responsibility to the Highest, and I too acknowledge that I am bound to the ethical standards expressed in the Ten Commandments. It may be that I do this for reasons somewhat different from those you Christians put forth. I want nothing to do, for example, with any idea of reward in heaven, upon which you church people set such great store. Nor do I want my contributions of time and money to be called 'alms,' as they are spoken of in your holy books. But in *practice* it all amounts to the same thing. 'I accept the Christian ethic fully and completely.' "

Now isn't it a very strange thing that in the Sermon on the Mount and especially in the very passage of the Sermon on the Mount which we have just read there is really very little or nothing at all said about this Christian ethic and that it deals with a totally different theme?

Obviously there must be something behind this, and it is no mere chance that right here Jesus does *not* set up any rules for ethical conduct, that he does *not*, for example, say: You should prove your love for your neighbor by *deeds*, by making sacrifices for him and being willing to make any contribution to him. Instead he says, "*Beware* of practicing your piety before men."

This cry "Beware," "Look out" reminds me of the warning calls I used to hear when we had to walk the dark, unlighted streets at night, when suddenly a trench or a stone or tangle of roots lay at my feet and I might have stumbled and fallen. The warning cry doubtless has the same meaning here. I can trip on a good deed, I can stumble over my Christian ethics and break my "spiritual" neck.

There are two things that are characteristic in this warning of Jesus. First, it is simply assumed as a matter of course that good works will be done and that they need not be made the subject of an express command. Jesus is here addressing himself to people who wish to live under the eye of God, who have had some experience of his mercy and therefore know that this mercy must flow through them to their neighbor, and hence that it cannot be hoarded within them like a dead pool with no outlet. The question whether one should or should not give alms is no problem at all to such people. Luther once said that there is no need to *command* a stone lying in the sun to become warm; it becomes so of itself. That's why Jesus here gives us no so-called moral commandment.

The second characteristic lies in the fact that, though Jesus tells us that there is no question about *whether* you should do good works, it is the good works *themselves* which are a problem. They are literally loaded with dangerous potentialities. They are strewn with roots and stones and it is surely a real miracle of God if you do not trip over them and fall miserably. That's why Jesus utters this warning cry: "Beware, beware! You are still not out of the woods when you have finally succeeded in wringing from your heart a contribution to some good cause or given a room to a homeless refugee or given your valuable time to someone who needs you. No, then the real danger is just beginning! I am afraid that you may drain out all the value of your so-called good works by being all too ready to blow the trumpet whenever you put your hand in your pocketbook and with a loud tantara call attention to it, if not the attention of others, at least your own: So, here comes Mr. So-and-So, what a noble fellow he is! You can even shed tears over your own goodness and kindness—it's true, isn't it? I am afraid your so-called good works may be depreciated by your looking too greedily for the reward you may get for them. Are not all of you secretly living in the thought pattern of reward and punishment? Are you not untiringly at work, say when hard reverses come, reckoning up to God what he ought to do and how he ought to reward you, since, after all, you have done this and that for him? Is there not in all your good works a secret but very dubious speculation?" And as a matter of fact, do not all of us reckon a little, or perhaps a great deal, upon recognition by God and by men, upon prestige, honor, and a good reputation? Do we not all strut a bit upon a lighted stage and assume poses, because the good Lord and our neighbors and colleagues are sitting in the orchestra and we would like to have some applause and lots of flowers and handshakes?

When Bishop Galen writes in his "Testament" the moving statement that perhaps many people may admire his courage in standing up for his faith and his rectitude, but that only God knows the depth of his wretchedness, he was doubtless referring to this secret of the human heart.

Jesus hears the trumpets of our moral ostentation. He sees us flattering ourselves and marks the higgling and haggling of our hearts, and it makes him sad, for he sees his people coming to grief despite all their Christian ethics, no longer able to hear the warning cry of the Good Shepherd above the bugle sounds of their own self-satisfaction. That's why he cries out, "Beware, beware! Once you have begun to fulfill the commandments of God then the real problems begin, then comes the real danger."

How can we heed this warning cry of Jesus Christ? In this hour we are not going to rely upon our good conscience, our good will, and our ethical principles, however respectable they may be. We are going to try to hear the Shepherd's voice in the depths of our Christian life.

I was once taken care of by a nurse who did her work perfectly, punctually, and self-sacrificingly. For twenty years she worked only on the night shift. I asked her once whether this was not a great strain that would eventually wear her out and wondered how she found the strength to do it. With a radiant look in her eyes she replied, "Well, you see, every night I put in sets another jewel in my heavenly crown, and already I have 7,175 in a row."

Why was it that my gratitude suddenly vanished, that I could no longer believe in her love, and that all at once the feeling of security disappeared? When she set out to help me,

I felt, she was looking straight through me as if I were just so much air; her eyes were secretly fixed upon her crown in heaven, savoring its sparkling glory.

Isn't it a terrible thing that a person can despise and offend his neighbor at the same time he is doing something good and working for the favor of the Father? For this is obviously what this nurse was doing: the sick people she was caring for were means to gain her end. She did not look at them with the eyes of Jesus, who was moved to compassion by their misery, who never ceased to be troubled by the fact that the children of his Father in heaven were exposed to the destroying powers of sickness, suffering, and death, and who laid down his life to bring them into his Father's kingdom where there is no suffering and no death. No, this nurse was just "using" her patients as means and materials. She was entranced by the thought that by doing this valuable and excellent work—for naturally there can be no doubt that she was and is an excellent nurse—she was producing more and more proof of her qualifications and that her balance in the bank of heaven was constantly increasing.

We understand, then, why these people were called "hypocrites" by Jesus. Of course he meant this in a sense much deeper than our ordinary use of the term indicates. Generally we think of a hypocrite as someone who consciously acts in a dishonest way, who leads his fellows about by the nose. He may even be a swindler who takes a certain pleasure in wearing a pious cloak in order to gain credit with his honest fellow citizens and then cheat the daylights out of them. We always picture the hypocrite as the wolf who has put on his sheep's clothing and then gets tremendous amusement watching his bleating fellow creatures being taken in.

But that nurse and we too would strenuously object to being named in the same breath with such hypocrites and wolves in sheep's clothing. After all, we mean well. Our intentions are honest and we want to help. And I mean that seriously, without disparagement.

But Jesus means something deeper when he uses the term hypocrite. He means that we ourselves can, without knowing it, fall into a disastrous contradiction with ourselves, that we can in all seriousness imagine that we are doing God a service when we help a person who may be disagreeable, tiresome, or utterly useless to us, while in reality we are only doing a service to ourselves, perhaps because we want to put this person under obligation to us or because we enjoy being generous for once and get a voluptuous pleasure in another's dependence upon us. Isn't it true that it makes us feel good to have in our hands another person's weal or woe? Nietzsche, as he so often does, reveals our most secret motives when he says: I would like to be the master of all men, but most of all God.

This hidden contradiction in our conduct—this is the real hypocrisy, the schizophrenia, the "split personality" of the natural man, who carries water on both shoulders and keeps looking both ways.

Often we do not realize this ourselves, and when we are addressed as hypocrites at the Last Judgment we shall reply in surprise, "What was that again?" and turn around, thinking it was surely the man behind us on whom the eye of God was resting.

One day it will be the delight of the satanic accuser to lay all this hypocrisy at our door, mine as well as yours. And the way he does it is classically described in the Book of Job. Job was a downright decent and honest man. He prayed and he worked. Not a single feature in his life is recorded which would give us the least justification for questioning his personal purity of character and good reputation. He really had a pure conscience, this good Job. And yet the secret prosecutor, the satanic accuser dared to contest the justification of this good conscience. He says to the Lord of heaven: "Sure, this Job is really a good man, I must admit it. But he is good only on one presupposition, namely, that because there is a higher moral world-order the good are rewarded and the wicked are punished, that real visible justice is at work in the world which one can take advantage of by being honest and good and serving God. But take away this assumption, take away as it were this view of life in which he operates, and you will see him lose his faith and instead of pious hymns only curses will issue from his mouth."

And then, when the devil was given permission to torment Job undeservedly, despite his outstanding goodness, in the face of all kinds of troubles, he actually succeeded. Job began to doubt God and his own piety. As soon as he found himself staring at grinning meaninglessness, as soon as his philosophy of a just order of life vanished like a bubble, his faith, too, collapsed. The dreadful thing about this story of Job is that the devil's corrosive skepticism turns out to be right. Job really did not lead a blameless life only for the greater glory of God; he was pious and good because he thought that "God does not allow the wicked to enslave the good," and therefore that if a man is good he will have more freedom and happiness in life.

There it is again, you see, this hidden hypocrisy, that hypocrisy that shows us that there is no relying on Job, no relying on our conscience. For our conscience—insofar as we take it even half way seriously—tends to defend and relieve us, constantly reassuring us that we have done right and that God's blessing cannot fail to come to us. When it comes to the ultimate things the conscience fails. It is by no means the voice of God. I should like to know who invented this pious legend. A conscience which is not bound to God's Word is a dangerous will-o'-the-wisp and an inexhaustible mine of self-righteousness. It is an all too flattering and optimistic lawyer for the self.

And therefore one thing is sure: in the struggle between the accusations of the devil and the defense of the conscience the devil *always* wins—simply because his eye is sharper than our conscience and he is not our friend. Our enemies *always* see our weaknesses more clearly than our friends. That's why we ought to stop at this point and listen to what the devil says, asking ourselves what charges he may have to prefer against us as our accuser at the Last Judgment. And the fact is that the satanic accuser does have a few truths to tell us which are not only bitter, but also—simply true.

Only when we have tasted this bitterness (and it's a sure thing that every one of us will have to taste it, for none can come to the throne of God without passing the accuser's chair) will we see what the apostle Paul saw and realized when he flung these words into the accuser's face: "Who shall bring any charge against God's elect? It is God who justifies; who is to condemn? It is Christ Jesus, who died, yes, who was raised from the dead, who is at the right hand of God, who indeed intercedes for us" (Rom. 8:33-34). Do you understand what is happening in these words?

Paul is not appealing to his good conscience as the accuser whispers to the throne of God, "Here comes another hypocrite, here comes the archhypocrite Paul!" No, what he is saying is this: "It may well be that this hypocrisy is in me too; God alone knows my secret faults and hidden motives. But I am no longer the hypocrite Paul. I am Jesus' yokefellow, and for this my Savior has taken upon his shoulders all my vices and my shortcomings. He died for this, and, behold, I come in the name of his 'blood and righteousness,' which is my 'beauty, my glorious dress.' Let no man trouble me; for I bear on my body the marks of the Lord Jesus. So, my accuser, what do you think you can do? Everything you lay to my charge no longer affects me, even though it be true. For I myself am no longer the one you mean. You would be right if I came in my *own* name, but I do not come in my own name, but in the name of him who loved me and give himself for me. If you ever succeed in arguing away the Cross of Calvary, I'll be yours lock, stock and barrel. But *that's* just what you will never be able to do. The Crucified is stronger than you, and his blood cleanses me from all sin. And that's why you *have* to let me get past to the Father." So speaks Paul as he turns to the accuser.

But now look—as the accuser is stricken to silence (when Paul speaks so and I may borrow his words) the Father is already stretching out his hands to me. For he who sits at his right hand in the glory of power and majesty has confirmed everything I have said: "All those whom thou hast given to me, Father, I have protected—and behold, dear Father, this man too is one of these my brethren." *These* are the words that sound from the right hand of God's throne.

What a comfort it is that here and now we should be hearing about that dark chapter in our life, our secret hypocrisy, from the same lips that will one day speak these comforting, succoring words at the Last Judgment! For here in the Sermon on the Mount Jesus Christ is saying exactly what the devil is saying to us.

For Jesus is the only one who knows us as well and even better than the devil, in any case, better than we know ourselves. "He knew what was in man" (John 2:25). But how different it is when *he* says it and at the same time lays a kind and healing hand upon this wound in our hearts. How different it sounds when it is *he* who says "Beware" to us. In it is the concern and pain of one who is anxious for his own. And because we sense this concern, we are willing to let him tell the truth to us. The inner opposition to the truth that wells up when the devil says it breaks down within us. What a wonderful thing it is to find all our opposition breaking down in the presence of Jesus, because we know he will not let us lie in shattered defeat, but will lift us up. And the worse we are the more he loves us.

But then even so, a grave doubt comes to our minds. Did not Jesus himself help at least a little to bring into being this hypocrisy in our hearts, this terrible conflict with ourselves? Does not he himself speak here and in other places of the *reward* which we shall receive? And by speaking of this idea of reward, does he not contribute fatally to our tendency to turn away from our neighbor and his need and to keep looking out for our heavenly bank account? Ought one not to do the good "for its own sake"? And here we find Jesus Christ *himself* talking about reward. How then can we blame that nurse for not caring for the sick simply out of compassion and rather using them as means to an end? Immanuel Kant, the great ethical thinker, once said that the greatest immorality was for me to use another person as a means to an end. Prostitution is immoral because here a living person created by God is used as a means to the end of satisfying lust. A social order is immoral when it makes possible the accumulation of power and wealth at the expense of others who are nothing more than slaves, and instead of being respected as living persons are regarded only as things, as means of production. And the most refined and subtle form of immorality appears when I help another person merely because I am selfishly seeking my own personal salvation, seeking to build up my own account in heaven. So this is a very real difficulty, is it not, to see Jesus at least failing to prevent our slipping into this immorality by way of his idea of reward?

What, then, does Jesus mean when he says that our helpful concern for our neighbor has value and that it is "rewarding"? *

He gives us a very clear answer in his description of the Last Judgment (Matt. 25:31). At this Last Judgment he will remind us that he was constantly walking this earth as the

* Here we return to a thought in our first chapter and carry it further. What we are confronted with here is a very important and constantly recurring objection that is made by ethical idealism.

hidden Christ, meeting us again and again in the hungry, the homeless, the lonely, the imprisoned and destitute. "As you did it to one of the least of these my brethren, you did it to me."

I venture to ask this question: Is there any way of showing a person more respect than to see in him the hidden Savior, the brother of the Lord? Can I ever put myself above the poorest and most despised of men, can I ever pride myself above another who needs my help and feel that I can be a patronizing possessor as long as the Savior takes these old and weak and "useless" ones under his protection, indeed, literally identifies himself with them? Is there any dignity higher than the dignity given to man by the Savior? It is like the dignity of a poor, yellowed photograph I may find among my mother's mementos. It too has no material value whatsoever and no artistic significance. But the fact that my mother's eyes rested upon this trifling picture, the fact that it stood perhaps on her sewing table makes it infinitely valuable to me. And so men too acquire their value from the fact that the eyes of the Lord rest upon them and Jesus thinks of them with love.

It's true, isn't it; we must have radically misunderstood what Jesus means here by "reward" if we could think that our neighbor could ever become a means to an end and be used merely to increase our bank account in heaven. We must have missed the meaning of reward altogether if we could suppose even for a moment that the nurse we spoke about could count upon it.

When Christ speaks of reward he uses the word quite simply in order to express the quality of an act and make us ask whether and why our act is "worthwhile," whether it "pays," whether it is "rewarding." And in this sense no man who is serious about what he does can avoid the question of reward. For even the person who does something for its own sake still cherishes the opinion that it "pays," that it is "rewarding"—simply because the *thing* itself is so important and rewarding. Even the idealist, who quite simply says it is the destiny of man to act morally without looking for reward and profit (that, for example, as a soldier he should be brave, as a nurse he should watch over the sick, that when his neighbor's house is on fire he should help, and give his second coat when his neighbor has none at all), even the idealist regards himself as being rewarded for his act. In this case the reward lies in the very fact that when he thus sacrifices himself and his means he is being true to this destiny, this deepest meaning and purpose of his life. Thus Walter Flex once said that the real happiness of his life was that for him thought and action were in harmony and that he was permitted to *live out* his conviction that to be really human demands sacrifice and devotion. So you see, this very harmony makes life *rewarding*.

So here again we see what we have already seen in a similar connection: the question of reward crops up in *every* view of life; there is no thought and action in which it is not constantly present.

Therefore the problem must be posed in a different way. We must ask: In *what* does the reward of helping our neighbor, making sacrifices, and giving ourselves wholly to him consist? The reward, the meaning of our love for our neighbor consists in the fact that we do it for *God's* sake, that we do it simply *because* he desires to meet us in the poorest of the poor: "Whatever your task, work heartily, as serving the Lord and not men." And because we do it for *his* sake, for the sake of his holy sacrifice, and hence because we do it for the sake of the great price with which he purchased even the poorest and least worthy, we grow ever more deeply into his fellowship as we love and give sacrifice. So more and more do we become branches on this Vine.

This fact alone that we are permitted to become members of his body, companions of Jesus, whom he leads through the world, through sin and need, and whom he will never forsake in this life or the next, this and this alone is our "shield and great reward" (Gen. 15:1). That's why our deeds are "rewarding," that's why they have meaning. This is my reward, and *not* the paltry jewels my pious flesh would like to accumulate. God does not reward us with things (and certainly not with such a monstrosity as a big cumbrous crown); he rather rewards us with his heart.

In his *Commentary on Romans,* Luther subjected himself to a mighty test whether there might be hidden egotistical motives even in *this* idea of reward, and in doing so he set down something like the following thoughts (I have already referred to them above): It may be that I want only to enjoy the felicity of thy nearness, O God, and therefore that everything I do, including my love for my neighbor and my worship of God, indeed, even my faith and trust, is not done to thy glory at all, but rather because I only want to enjoy the noble felicity of thy fellowship, and therefore it may be that I am seeking, not *thee,* but *myself.* Therefore I am ready to put myself to a test, O God: Do thou condemn me to the depths of hell, despite my worship and my brotherly love, indeed, despite my faith in the wounds of Jesus; and I will accept even this disappointment of my faith without murmuring and will praise thee even in the depths of hell. Even there will I raise a sign that thou canst deal with me as thou wilt. Even there will I prove that I did not love thee for the sake of any reward. . . . But even as I ponder all this and contemplate this extreme trial of faith, I know all the time that thou wilt not leave me in hell, but wilt clasp to thy heart as thy child him who dares this utmost leap of faith.*

* Gottfried Keller in his *Green Henry* realized in his own way the inescapability of the concept of reward. "It has happened to me to repulse a poor man on the street because, even while I wanted to give him something, I was thinking at the same time of God's approval, and did not want to act in my own self-interest. Then, however, I felt sorry for the poor man, I ran back; but while I was running back, my very compassion seemed to me too much of an affectation." [Gottfried Keller, *Green Henry,* trans. A. M. Holt (N.Y.: Grove Press, 1960), pp. 25 f.]

Here it is made clear in an ultimate, unconditional, and as it were extreme way what reward means in the New Testament. It means that I can rely utterly upon the promise and the mercy of God, knowing that God will never let me down and that even in my most devout thoughts I need not seek to gain my own interests.

Even if I compelled myself to think, as it were by an intellectual act of violence, that God would condemn me to the depths of hell, regardless of all my faith, if I tried in this extremely violent way to get away from the idea of reward, then even in this *notional* hell the mercy of God would be greater than my heart, even there his royal reward would be awaiting me. And if I cast aside all my calculations and speculations, even if I discounted all the claims of which I am solemnly assured by God's own Word and any appeal to my own faith, then even in this *ultimate* nakedness and vulnerability I would still be surprised to find God throwing his "glorious dress" about my nakedness, eager to be my shield and great reward, and thus that I shall still be his child and therefore will be rewarded beyond all that we ask or think.

And now that we have thought this through together, I ask you, can the word "alms" still have the "smack" which it now has in our imagination? We tend to think of alms as a gift that is given condescendingly. We think of them as crumbs which we as lords let fall from our table. And an "almsman" or receiver of alms is likely to be thought of as something like a little dog that greedily snaps them up and is dependent upon our generosity.

But as soon as we put it in this way—and admittedly it is a caricature—we find that these alms can become a sign of what God does for *us*. For just as the needy person often appears to our proud imagination to be somebody who has no claim at all upon us and is dependent upon our grace and compassion, so this is *actually* and without any imagination our situation before

God. In any case, *he* certainly does not find us "lovable," "worthy of his love"—and yet he loves us *nevertheless*. We have no bill to present, but nevertheless, *he* pays our debts.

We crucify the Savior and do so every day of our lives, for we want to be our own masters; but *he* takes this cross, which we ourselves raised up, and raises it above us, turning the very sign of our opposition into a banner of peace.

Once we have discovered, then, that ever since the Fall every one of us, you and I included, are all paupers and almsmen of God, must not our own almsgiving suddenly appear in a totally different light? The people to whom we give alms also sense very clearly whether we are acting like little tin gods, graciously condescending to bestow a charitable gift or whether we are giving as those who themselves have received abundantly and now are passing it on to others in gratitude and humiliation.

Only he who *himself* has received mercy can really give and help others without humiliating and dishonoring them. Hence the real gift—and I mean by this the upbuilding, helping gift, the royal sign of mercy—also does not flow from our proud hands, carelessly dropping the alms. It flows from the quiet chamber in which we give thanks to God for all the undeserved good things in our life which he has given to us, all the way from the great spiritual gift of being permitted to be his children down to food and drink and shoes and clothing which still are ours to enjoy.

So let us be givers and sacrificers and thus messengers of this mercy of God. Let us be brothers to the least of these brethren, in order that our Brother, Jesus Christ may meet us in them. Then this will be our shield and great reward.

Beware, take care, give heed to your alms and your Christian ethics! You can meet and find your *Savior* in your brother man, or you can lose your place in the Father's house, despite your piety and your rectitude. "You were bought with a price; do not become slaves of men" (I Cor. 7:23).

8

Talking About God or With God?

"And when you pray, you must not be like the hypocrites; for they love to stand and pray in the synagogues and at the street corners, that they may be seen by men. Truly, I say to you, they have their reward. But when you pray, go into your room and shut the door and pray to your Father who is in secret; and your Father who sees in secret will reward you.

"And in praying do not heap up empty phrases as the Gentiles do; for they think that they will be heard for their many words. Do not be like them, for your Father knows what you need before you ask him."   —*Matthew 6:5-8*

Not long ago I read again in the well-known autobiography of Friedrich von Bodelschwingh the chapter in which he gives his account of the death of his four children one after another within two weeks, leaving the stricken parents in dreadful loneliness.

The thing in this account that affects one so deeply is not so much the terrible event itself, though any father who had little children of his own and saw them exposed hour by hour to the deadly menace of the bombing raids would surely be deeply moved by this account of the Grim Reaper's assault upon these innocent, hardly opened blooms of childhood.

Far more moving in this account is the way in which Bodelschwingh writes about the death of these four little children, the way in which he tells how he committed each one of these beloved children to the fatherly hands of God and also how they too looked longingly to their Shepherd as "Jesus' little lambs."

In the last analysis what is it that is so moving in this story?

I think it is this: that even in the worst moments of this truly ghastly trial of faith Father Bodelschwingh never lost contact with God, that his childlike conversation with the Father in heaven never ceased, and hence that never for a moment did this conversation with God appear to yield to that dumb, leaden silence which many of us know from the darkest days of our life.

It can also be expressed negatively: it is true that Bodelschwingh said later that when this happened he learned for the first time how *hard* God can be; but nevertheless he apparently never asked "How can God allow such a thing to happen?" or "Why should God do this to me?"

That is to say that anybody who asks that question is no longer speaking *with* God, but only *about* God. What he is doing is making him the topic of a discussion, turning him into a matter of debate, the undertone and implication of which is expressed in words like this: "Let's just look at this God a little more closely. Is a person really expected to be able to believe a thing like that?" And then, of course, what happens is what happens in almost every debate: the subject is talked to pieces and God melts away in one's hands, choked to death in a lot of words—at least so far as he is *our* God.

Characteristically, this fearful moment of doubt and deicide did *not* occur at this crisis in Bodelschwingh's life, for he did not talk *about* God and he turned the very dread itself into a prayer. And in this he was following the example of the crucified Savior. For even when Jesus cried out in the agony of death, "My God, my God, why hast thou forsaken me?" this has nothing to do with the modern doubt, which sounds so similar to it, because it too asks the question "Why" and yet asks it so differently. For in reality it only talks *about* God and cries out *about* God, and in that very act *cries him down,* so that he is no longer heard.

For even in this uttermost depth of trial the Crucified still addressed his Father in *prayer:* "My God, my God . . . ," and this cry of terrible torment is clothed in the words of the Old Testament. He spoke to the Father as it were in the Father's own words. So close to the Father's side is he even *here*—even in this extreme darkness when the face of the Father seemed to have vanished utterly.

Why do I mention all this? Simply because it teaches us to understand the opening words of our text. For it begins with the words, "When, or whenever, you pray. . . ." If I am catching the sense of this, Jesus is here alluding to the fact that our praying is not a matter of course, but that we talk more *about* God and would rather talk *about* God than *with* him. For what is referred to here is not merely a fixed time of prayer in the sense of "When the time of your hour of prayer comes, you should do so and so." It is rather a *conditional clause:* if it should come to the point (come to the point *at all*) where you pray (even if this "at all" is as it were guaranteed by set rules and times of prayer), then you should do this or that.

Prayer is therefore not a self-evident, automatic thing. To say that we pray "always" and are "always" in communication with the Father is out of the question. With us prayer is more or less an exceptional thing. It is an event that occurs from time to time and, so to speak, requires definite conditions.

Why is this? Why is it that we have so much trouble with our prayer life, instead of finding in it the real substance and joy of our existence? Why is it that we have to *force* ourselves to keep company with the Father? Why is it that we are always so weary and indolent and that every silly newspaper, every vexation, or even every joy that comes our way is able to kill or crowd out our prayers, until finally we only talk *about* God and after a time even stop doing that? For anybody who once makes of God a mere topic usually turns after a time to more current and immediate topics.

The reason for this lies in the fact that prayer is no longer the native soil of our life, our home, whose air we desire to breathe. The world is our home—the world and all that fills us to bursting, the worries about money and food; the letter we receive or have to write; the dissensions with our colleagues; the concern about getting ahead in our business or profession; the cramped quarters we live in; the nervous tensions; the sleep that overpowers us at evening or the sleep we miss, when forced wakefulness drives us, not into reflection, but only into nervousness; this world that consumes and hounds us, keeping us vibrating no matter whether it is moving or stopping. This world has become our home, except that it is incapable of giving us the security of home.

So we have this dislocated feeling that the world of prayer is a strange and alien place, that we therefore need some kind of a push, a resolution, a positive force, in order to muster up the desire to pray and to tear ourselves away from our home in the world.

How different was Jesus' prayer! When he came to men to preach and to heal he came out of the homeland of prayer. What he said to men he had first talked over with the Father. He came out of this prayerful contact with the Father, where he was really at home, into the alien country of this world. And look at the tremendous difference between Jesus and us: with effort *we* rouse ourselves out of the consuming concerns of the world—"Whenever you pray"; whereas Jesus lives in prayer and, just the opposite from us, comes from prayer and enters *into* the concerns of this world. Here we begin to see what is lacking, how deeply estranged we are from the *real* life. We are amazed to hear what Luther, following in his

Lord's footsteps, somehow managed to do. He prayed from three to four hours every day, and he tells us that the great fullness of his life's work came out of these hours of quiet, whereas *we* would think just the opposite, namely, that these hours would be lost from the day's work and that in any case we today could never afford this loss of time.

Could it not be that the truth is quite different from what we think with all our shrewd and modern way of looking at things? In any case, this is my experience: the shorter and more hurried our prayer time becomes, until finally it dwindles to a few seconds of reading the daily text, the more it actually becomes a burden, because these few seconds lack strength and savor, which means that they have no quietness in them and therefore no longer provide a sustaining foundation for the day—despite or just because of their brevity, which we think is so rational. This is the irony that mocks our rationalization of our prayer life and destroys it by the very means by which we try to salvage a tiny portion of our life for it.

We sober realists ought to be sober and realistic enough to know that this economy of time is deficit-spending economy; and in this vicious circle we grow more and more disinclined and averse to prayer.

When the devout man of the Old Testament offered an animal for sacrifice which was not free of blemishes his sacrifice was not accepted *at all*. The man who does not give to God the best hours of the day, the hours when he is most fresh and alert, but rather reads his mail or the newspaper first or indulges in his own pursuits, good or bad, which he thinks are more pressing, will receive nothing *at all* from his heavenly Father; he ought to keep his mouth shut altogether, because it will be shut for him anyhow.

Down underneath we also know very well that God does not have first place in our life—neither the first place in time at the beginning of the day nor the first place in the actual importance he has for our life. That's why we think that certain conditions have to be fulfilled in order that we may pray. Among these conditions we include, for example, the stipulation that we must first have time and quietness (though it is just the other way around—it is only in praying that we get this quietness!); and also that we must be in the *mood*, for which again we need leisure and quiet and above all the stimulus of some kind of solemn ceremony (perhaps a Christmas or Easter service) or some great moment in our life. But anybody who sets up conditions for God is off the track from the start and again had better keep his mouth shut. God gives himself only when we put ourselves unconditionally in his hands.

And here our text gives us the decisive direction. All this waiting for devout moods or moments when our hearts are so full of care and fear that we can hardly do anything else but pray, all this waiting for such moments is brushed aside by Jesus' repeated *command* to pray.

I should think that this could be a real comfort to all of us when our prayer life breaks down. As we find again and again that we are not in the mood or that we have other thoughts in our mind, and besides—we know the old routine by heart—we have "no time," there comes to us the command *"Pray,"* "Seek ye my face" (Ps. 27:8). Now it is simply the Christian's *service*, the obligation, so to speak, of his office as a Christian, that he should pray—an obligation which, in exactly the same sense as our daily work, simply disregards the question whether we are in the mood to go to work tomorrow: "A job is a job."

And then, too, what a liberation this command can be when we are in a state of doubt and dispute with God, tormented by the thought that prayer may have no meaning at all, that—as Rilke once said in another connection—the whole thing is like calling on a telephone when nobody ever answers at the other end, that it is therefore utterly senseless to attempt to intervene by prayer in the natural, inevitable course of a disease like cancer. Are not all of us staring, like a rabbit held spellbound by a serpent's eyes, into the dreadful fate in store for us in the atomic age, the massing clouds of great cosmic catastrophes that threaten to discharge upon our heads? Have not all of us, down in the secret corners of our hearts, become a bit fatalistic and so tend to forego the feeble gesture of prayer, which, after all, is only the whimpering of a child in a storm and does not avert the storm anyhow?

What a comfort it is then simply to be lifted above these doubts and hesitations by a command, just as a soldier knows that he is in duty bound by a command, even when he does not understand the command. Often we do not understand the mystery of prayer theoretically, and discussions about it are pretty futile. But we learn it in obedience and in the practice of it, just as we learn to understand the Lord better the more we follow him; and we misunderstand him more the more we insist upon understanding beforehand "why" this discipleship is justified and worth while.

So prayer is not a matter of our mood and inclination; it is a matter of a command. But we must remember that he who gives a command thereby assumes full responsibility for it. And Jesus gave the command. So we can take him at his word, and, as Luther said, we should "throw the whole sackful of his promises at his feet." We do not come merely in our own name —good heavens, who are *we*, we who are drunk with hope, plagued by fear, and undermined by doubt; how could *we* ever rise above this sea of madness, how could we ever break through this blockade in our life?—I say, we come, not in our own name, but in the name of the Lord Jesus. We come in his name, not only because he has commanded us to pray, but because through his death and resurrection he has made us again children of his Father and therefore has given us the right to speak as children and to trust in his suffering and death.

Then Jesus gives us still another indication of how little all this depends upon us alone and our mood. He says, "When you pray, go into your room and shut the door." This we visualize perhaps as a simple but solemn room, possibly furnished with a cross, a gold-edged Bible on a table, and a *prie-dieu*. But what Jesus means is the storeroom outside of the house, a very unsolemn and very unreligious and very prosaic place. This may indicate how unnecessary it is for us to climb up upon a special pedestal and reach a particular mood in order to find the Father. We can come just as we are—simply because God came to *us* first in the Christmas Child and because his coming too was very prosaic and unsolemn. There is only *one* respect in which the quiet room will help us to pray, and that is that we can be alone with God and that this aloneness will not be disturbed by pious play acting or by things and people, impressions and thoughts that press in on us from all sides. We should therefore in all earnestness see to it that we keep the hour of prayer undisturbed. There is nothing more wonderful than this hour of quiet. And the devil operates far less with doubts and evil thoughts than with the harassing maneuvers of petty trivialities. He works through haste and restless thoughts, through crowded conditions which make it almost impossible to find such a quiet place. And I venture to say that modern, urban man's lack of time and the overcrowded housing conditions provide the devil with more welcome opportunities than all the Feuerbachs and Nietzsches and anti-Christian propagandists put together. The quiet room is one of the most important strategic points in the confusion of our time; for he who has lost sight of *God* (and only here will he find him) no longer knows how to cope with the world. How can one structure a world when one has stopped up the springs of blessing and cut off communications with him who has overcome the world?

Then Jesus mentions still another, last difficulty about prayer that disturbs our contact with God. It appears in our heaping up empty phrases like the pagans who think they will be heard for their many words.

Actually, the two most dangerous causes of disease in our prayer life are either that we use *too few* words because our contingent of thoughts and resolves runs out, having already been spent on people and things, or that we use *too many* words because we do not trust anything to God.

So it is elsewhere in life too: when a person who wants to obtain something from us uses a great plethora of words there are usually two possible explanations for his doing so.

The *first* is that he has a bad conscience and also has a lot to cover up with his many words. We have to watch out that he does not covertly bring us around to something quite different from what he so emphatically insists is his purpose.

So Jesus is quite right to distrust the pious talkers: may not they too be wanting something quite different from what they say? They declare that what they want is contact with the Father, his blessing and giving hand. But in reality they are not concerned about that hand at all, but as Walter Flex once said, only about the pennies in that hand. In their trouble or in their desires they want to *gain* something from him, they want him as a means to an end, and when he has helped them they run away, simply because the means has performed its function and is dismissed with favor or disfavor. It is of these people—are we among them too?—that Jesus was thinking with deep sadness when he said after the miraculous feeding of the five thousand (John 6:26): You seek me, not because you saw signs (i.e., you seek me, not because I revealed myself to you as your Savior in the miracle of the feeding and because you were given a glimpse into my heart and my loving concern for you), but because you ate your fill of the bread. No sooner are your stomachs filled than you forget me, and if you say a prayer of thanksgiving at all, your "Amen" sounds more like

"Boy, am I stuffed"! This is what you are trying to cover up with your many words. O you fools, seeking the gifts and not the Giver!

Was not Jesus talking about you and me when he said this? How passionately we prayed as the bombs whistled down upon our roofs and how feeble our thanks when the "All Clear" came! The reason for it was that we were concerned only about our little bit of life and not about his kindly heart, watching over us and stationing his angels like a guard around us.

It was probably because the person who prays is thus concerned first of all to gain contact with the Father and to reach out for his hand that the ancient prayers of the church were accustomed to begin with a long, detailed address. There was a time when I did not understand this and was even critical of it, for I felt that one would be so exhausted by these long addresses that one could hardly take in the real substance of the prayer. But perhaps now we understand what the fathers were trying to achieve through these "long-winded" addresses and why this may also give us a pointer for our own praying. The fathers were concerned not merely to express their needs and hopes in prayer, but above all to establish contact with that last court of appeal which they were approaching with these needs and hopes. Otherwise we may be all too apt to dwell upon the fears and hopes that fill our hearts and our prayer will never get us free from ourselves, because the "addressee" has never been found at all, indeed, has never even been approached.

Then there is a *second* explanation why a person may overwhelm us with a plethora of words when he wishes to gain something from us. His verbosity may be due to the fact that he *distrusts* us. He steps on the accelerator, as it were, in order to set us moving, because he thinks, rightly or wrongly, that we are too inert to move of ourselves. Or he may use a lot of words and graphic descriptions as tearjerkers in order to move us, because he thinks we have a stony and pitiless heart.

Or he may be desperately trying to make us understand his situation, because he assumes that we are uncomprehending and cold.

And this is exactly what Jesus says of those who "heap up empty phrases" in their prayers. They, too, step on the accelerator because they think they have to get things moving themselves, because they do not really believe that God has been thinking about us before we even began to think. They, too, work on the tear glands in their prayers, because they do not believe in the Father's measureless mercy. What they are practicing is work-righteousness in the form of prayer.

And therefore because we are among these people who distrust God and cannot get away from our activism even in prayer and thus cannot bring ourselves simply to let ourselves *fall* into God's hands, Jesus is calling out to *us*:

"Your Father knows what you need before you ask him. He is already there, even *before* your need comes. He is already there, ahead of the waves that threaten to engulf you. I, your Savior, am already there, before your sins; you have only to claim what lies ready for you to use. For the blessing and the help and the salvation are there, ready at hand. Don't you see that all your efforts, your chattering of empty phrases, your crying is like battering down a door that is already open? Don't you see what a terrible distrust this is of him who has opened the door and is waiting for you, as did the father of the prodigal son? What you are doing in these furious prayers is like writing threatening letters to your Father, telling him he is obligated to help you, when all the while this Father is thinking of you day and night and waiting for the first sign that you are willing to come home. When you know that someone loves you and is near to you, it does not require many words, but only a quiet sign, a glance, a little suggestion, and he will understand. Should it be any different with your Father? Your Father 'who knows what you need before you ask him'?"

These are precisely the words that bring a great calm to our prayers. We do not need to utter any long and well-phrased speeches; God understands even a sigh or a groan. He also understands the crude and halting words—simply because he loves us and knows us better than we know ourselves. And the groans of a dying child of God, who can no longer speak and is already beyond the zone in which human words count, are more precious to him than all the calculating prayer-rhetoric of many a devout person and many a shrewd and "religious" worldling.

But all this is true only on one condition, and that is that we come in the name of him who taught us to pray in this way. How else could we ever arrive at the acceptance of the fact that a Father hears us, that he takes an interest in us, listens for our sighs, and desires to make his dwelling place in our poor chamber? The people who keep telling us Christians that it is presumptuous of us to bother God with our trivialities, that we are rating ourselves altogether too high when we do this and making of God an all too human person, these critics are actually right. If we did not recognize in Christ the fatherly heart of God; if we did not see in him that divine downward pull that keeps drawing God to broken and contrite hearts, to the poor in spirit, to widows and orphans, the sick and the destitute, in a word, to his lost and beloved children; if we did not know the dark night of the Cross, in which the Son of God allowed himself to be plunged to the abyss of hell, compared with which the most cruel depths of human woe are but as green valleys, *then*, yes, it would of course be better if we kept quiet, because it is more courageous to stand up and bear adversity than to console oneself with illusions and pious romanticism.

But this Savior *has* appeared, the door to the Father's house *is* open, and now nothing can separate us from the love of God.

I said a moment ago that we are commanded to pray, but having said that, this last thing must be added. Such a command

and task would be meaningless if the really clinching thing in all this were not the *gift*, which means that we are given to know that in Jesus Christ we have the joyful and indescribable surprise of knowing that we have a Father who loves us, that there is someone upon whom we can cast all our cares, that there are watching over us eyes that see all the misery and the longing, that there are ears listening to us that can interpret the sighs and groans.

"Out of the depths I cry to thee, O Lord!" Yes, now I really can do this, since all this is true. Blessed be he who can hear us because he himself is beside us in whatever depths from which we may cry and pray! His ear is inclined to our voice and his heart is marvelously ready to hear, to understand, and to help "more abundantly than all that we ask or think."

Don't you see: we are being called by name, and now we need only to answer, now we need only to speak out and cry out with all our strength, "Here I am!"

This answering to that *call*, which has already come to us— that's what prayer is.

And now let us trust with all our hearts that there is a Father who has called to us, and then stride bravely into the dark, never ceasing to call back to him, perhaps as Peter cried when he threatened to sink into the sea—that's what faith is.

9

Homecoming

"And when you fast, do not look dismal, like the hypocrites, for they disfigure their faces that their fasting may be seen by men. Truly, I say to you, they have their reward. But when you fast, anoint your head and wash your face, that your fasting may not be seen by men but by your Father who is in secret; and your Father who sees in secret will reward you." —*Matthew 6:16-18*

There was a great and pathetic amount of fasting in our country in the years immediately following the war. Almost every one of us has painfully learned to know what it is. Countless mothers know what it meant to hear the children cry for bread when there was none to be had. The columns of our newspapers contained pitiful accounts of people going hungry. There was no talk about anointing one's head, but a lot about tightening one's belt. There was no talk about religious discipline, but a lot about the breakdown of morals and the black market. There was no talk about cheerful asceticism, but a lot about the dreadful duress that had been laid upon physical existence, in whose deadly embrace all nobler human impulses gave way to the naked and brutal struggle for existence.

Well now, shall I talk about the blessing of hunger and try to find the good side of this situation of self-restraint and abstinence, instead of all of us getting together and doing everything we can to break the reign of hunger in the world? Shall

I gush and rave about starvation being a devout training for heaven, instead of helping our hungry neighbors, right here and now?

I do not believe that this religious glorification of hunger is in accord with the mind of him who taught us to pray for our daily bread, who fed the hungry and laid his hands upon the sufferers in order that they might be set straight again. He made food and clothing objects for which we are to pray and give thanks, not a matter of abstinence and self-denial. And how could we seriously give thanks and pray for something which we do not at the same time seek to gain with all the strength we have?

It is perfectly clear what the Lord, who is a Savior of souls and bodies, is requiring of us now—not to talk about the blessing of hunger, but rather to help the hungry, because they are his brethren: *I* am hungry, are you feeding Me? *I* am the one who is gazing at you from the faces of these emaciated, mortally weakened people; will you help Me?

But in reality our text has in it a quite different question. Our text speaks of the earnestness of repentance, of a break with the world, and the overcoming of that which enslaves us and prevents us from doing so. And one of these is the stomach, both a full *and* an empty stomach. All this Jesus drives home by reference to the way in which repentance was practiced at that time, especially the practice of fasting. But the fasting is not the main thing, but only a means of illustration. The main thing is repentance. What does this mean?

At bottom repentance means simply to turn around, to turn around and go back home. And that again strikes the same note that runs through the whole Sermon on the Mount. This theme says that what is at stake in what Jesus wants of us is *not* that he wants to "enrich" our lives by adding to it religion and the life to come. So he is often understood and misunderstood. People say, for example, that there is an economic, a cultural, and a political area in our life, but that there is also a religious realm, and woe to the statesman who does not take this area into his calculations. Then, they say, he is overlooking an important factor in human leadership. He is not taking into account certain spiritual energies which can only be tapped and mobilized on the basis of religion. The man who is only a politician is a bad politician; but he can learn something from Christ about this important quality of the religious element, for nobody ever expressed himself as clearly and impressively about this as did Jesus Christ. Some people are even saying that even the atheistic countries have rediscovered the so-called religious potential and are beginning again to recognize it.

But how pitifully we should misunderstand our Lord if we were to believe that he merely intended to add to the other areas of life and our other needs a further sector, namely the religious sphere with its special view of life and its religious needs! Then discipleship would be an easy matter. Then all you would have to do is to learn a few things in addition to what you already know, such as what happens to us after death (which we did not know before but which presumably we learn from the Bible), what spiritual energies this so-called faith can release, and finally, how we can overcome all our complexes and inner tensions with the aid of the peace of mind that can be obtained in this additional sector in our life.

But now I ask you: Do these disciples, do all these people in the New Testament who came under the power of Jesus Christ look even remotely as if they had merely been enriched by that kind of experience, as if their mental horizon had merely been enlarged to include the religious side of life? Is not what they experienced in Jesus something far less innocuous than that? Are not all of them people who have been flung off their course by a storm and struck down by lightning? Are they not people for whom the door of their past life, indeed, the mighty door of the world itself, has been slammed shut and who now see that they have been set down in a totally new dimension in which they live according to laws that are completely different from what they were before? In a dimension in which they must now consider as small and mere refuse what formerly was the great thing that had first place in their life? In which they must burn up what formerly they reverenced, and reverence what formerly they cast into the fire (Acts 19:19)?

Are not all these people of the New Testament gazing at this shut door in deep astonishment, struck almost numb and dumb with amazement that the old has really passed away and the new has come, that they have been born again, that their former life, in which they loved and hated, ate and drank and married, in which they were interested and indifferent, has passed away like an unreal dream, whereas now for the first time the hour of truth and fact and reality has dawned upon them? Does not every Christian experience exactly the same amazement?

What they had and what we all experience in Jesus Christ is no mere extension or addition to our life, but rather a new life before which the old life fades away and is canceled out. This is no mere problem of addition in which a new area, the religious area, is annexed to our previous life. No, it is an act of tremendous demolition and reconstruction on land that has been leveled to the ground in the midst of pain and terror, land that is cluttered with the castles, citadels, and gardens of our old life.

But now, how does this decisive event, which we have just described as a turning around, a revaluation, a slamming of a door, a leveling, really come about?

Does this turning away from the old life come about through a person's becoming fed up and disgusted with himself, realizing his emptiness, and growing sick of it? After all, there are all kinds of "philosophers of disgust." They are called pessimists, and they say, openly or indirectly, that life is a desert and a pigsty. But what they mean is another kind of disgust; it is a loathing that never really frees a person from what disgusts him, but only drives him deeper and literally compels him to wallow in cynicism, in the nothingness of life, in the great wound of the world's anxiety. From this kind of disgust comes only resignation with no homecoming, a dreary nihilistic despair.

One need only to look at the prodigal son to sense the fresh, the totally different air that blows in the New Testament. How did it come about that he suddenly broke away from the desert and the pigsty? Was it because it stank to high heaven? Was it because he had had enough of the farmer who gave him only husks to eat? Was it because he was sick and tired of his miserable standard of living? None of this would have driven him to make a break; he would probably have hanged himself and put an end to it in this way.

But that he sprang to his feet and began to run, began to run home, to his father; that a feeling of strength swept through him and he became active—this was because suddenly the vision of his father's house loomed up in his soul and he saw in spirit the father waving and beckoning to him; and suddenly he knew and was sure that the father would accept him if he went. Sure, he was fed up with the far country, the trumpery, the sounding brass and tinkling cymbals of the taverns, which once he had taken so terribly seriously. But this was only incidental. The main thing was simply the joy of realizing: I can go home again! That's why repentance is repeatedly described as joy; and it was a sign that a man was rejoicing when he anointed his head.

Certainly the prodigal son would have looked with surprise at the mayor of his home town if he had said to him, "What's the matter, did they take your residence permit away from you, that all of a sudden you come back home?" The homecomer would certainly not have been at a loss for an answer: "What do you mean; do you think I'm here now because I was forbidden to stay in the far country? No, sir, it wasn't that at all.

It was my father's *offer*, my father's acceptance that brought me home." And if the mayor had said, "But the next time your father will certainly forbid you to go into the far country," the prodigal son would have laughed at him and said, "No need for prohibition any more; once a man knows what the peace and protection of the father's house means"—in other words, once one knows what fellowship with God and peace in Jesus Christ is—"he simply doesn't leave of his own accord."

Well, is it really true that a person never leaves again? Does a person really stay at home in the peace of the Father once he has come home, once he has been "converted"? Does all the rest of it proceed automatically, without any tensions or crises whatsoever? If the prodigal son had replied to the mayor as we have just said he would, would not this be incorrect? And this question brings us right to the center of our text.

For this text assumes and obviously agrees that it takes certain spiritual exercises and exertions, that it requires a spiritual discipline to come back home and to remain there. And part of this discipline or training may be fasting.

So this matter of coming home and remaining there is not so simple and automatic after all; and we can find evidence for this in other places in the New Testament. Thus Paul says, "I pommel my body and subdue it, lest after preaching to others I myself should be disqualified" (I Cor. 9:27). So it is possible, even after we have come home, to disqualify ourselves in a very subtle way. We can still, as it were, keep one foot in the far country. In another place Paul says: It is true that I am a free man; since I am a child in the father's house there is no restricting law. I can eat and drink, I can laugh and be merry, I can dance and sing, "but I will not be enslaved by anything" (I Cor. 6:12; 10:23). In the name of evangelical freedom bestowed upon me in the Father's house it is therefore possible for me to slip back into the far country inadvertently. And hence the First Epistle of Peter admonishes us, "Keep sane and sober for

your prayers," which means, after all, that when your nerves
are fevered, when the passions are excited, when your appetites
clamor for satisfaction, this is the very time when you do *not*
pray, this is when contact with the Father is broken.

So all this would certainly not make it appear that once a
man is in the Father's house he is safe and all the tempting
voices of the far country are silenced once and for all. On
the contrary, it sounds more like a warning, an alert, a call to
struggle and watchfulness. And this is precisely what Jesus is
saying: the peace of God is not life insurance! It is not something to sit on, but something you keep reaching out for constantly. And he who thinks that he stands—that he is standing,
for example, inside the threshold of the Father's house where
nothing can happen to him again—let him take heed lest he fall
and suddenly find himself outside again.

Now, perhaps some of you may say: Isn't this a terrible thing
you have just said? Are you saying that Jesus isn't strong enough
to banish this danger once and for all, once he has laid his hand
upon us? Is his blood, which he shed for me, too weak and in-
effectual to immunize me sufficiently? Is his Cross merely a
banknote without sound cover, instead of a sign of triumph,
a sign that all who embrace it are now inviolable and safe?

Well, it is a good thing to doubt and then to express our doubt
openly. For doubters are people who stretch out their hands
and therefore can be *taken* by this Hand.

That is to say that Jesus is so mighty that his very presence
brings all his enemies into concentrated attack, simply because
they realize that they are mortally threatened. Think of the
frenzy of the demonic spirits in the possessed when Jesus looks
upon them! Think of all the forces, even the mutually antago-
nistic forces like Herod and Pontius Pilate, that closed ranks
and joined together when it came to destroying him! Think
of the resistance and the exasperation that rise up against every
confessing Christian! And so it is within ourselves too; as soon

as we have given ourselves to Jesus Christ, the Adversary mobilizes every hostile force within us, from crude sensuality to the subtle doubts in our minds, in order to drive Jesus from the arena and conquer our hearts.

Of course the satanic strategy is far too cunning to limit itself to frontal attacks and to approach us with crude seductions. For as a rule frontal attacks can be detected before they are launched and one can prepare for them. Rather the Adversary usually begins in the secondary theaters of war. He pitches us, for example, into the state where we have a chronic lack of time, which on the surface seems to be a very ordinary affair that has little to do with spiritual things; but meanwhile this lack of time deprives us of time for prayer. Or he lays the morning paper on our breakfast table and it robs us of the quietness of prayer by involving us in the excitements of the day's events. Or he encompasses us with a thousand cares, whose ugly faces keep staring through our prayers as in a glass and thus become the real preoccupation of our hearts. Or he makes us champions of evangelical freedom and surreptitiously makes it a pretext for evil. All this makes it clear that the disciple of Jesus is being led into a more intensified struggle. For all this simply confronts him with tasks which he has to cope with day by day and deal with in a very practical way. It is a highly practical, matter-of-fact, clearly defined task to deal with lack of time, to prevent the daily newspaper from superseding the Bible, and to see to it that, though cares may flutter about our heads like gloomy birds, they do not build their nests there.

So the peace of God is no resting place free of struggle and temptation, but rather a struggle made all the more intense *because* Jesus is so mighty. Anybody who has so great a Lord as this also has the honor of having many enemies.

But then the worst danger in this battle is what the Lord in this text calls "hypocrisy." We have already had to speak about it in earlier parts of these talks. Hypocrisy is far more than a mere make-believe maneuver in which one makes a rather crude attempt to appear more devout than one really is. Here Jesus is undoubtedly speaking of *unconscious* hypocrisy. He is speaking of our worshiping God outwardly and without knowing it actually serving ourselves and the devil. Thus hypocrisy can be a horrible aberration in our life—poisoning it unwittingly at its deepest root.

In our text Jesus shows us how and when this happens. It happens when our life, including our inner life, is not lived in a primary relationship with God, in solitude with God alone, but is lived outwardly directed toward men, or when I am a spectator of my own piety. In other words, when this inner life, instead of being a "treasure in heaven" (Matt. 6:20), instead of being "hidden with Christ in God" (Col. 3:3), becomes something to be displayed in the show window of our life.

Now some of you may smile secretly and say to yourselves, "Well, that couldn't happen to me; I don't put on a dismal or a pious face, I don't stand or kneel in church saying my prayers too long and too conspicuously (which would be about the equivalent of praying at the street corners), nor am I what one could call a sanctimonious or a pious saint." Are you sure about that? Here again I can only warn that we tend to think of what happens here in our inner life as being something crude and clumsy. The nets with which the Adversary seeks to catch us are made of gossamer and almost invisible. Only in the light of Jesus Christ does their glint begin to betray them so that we recognize them for what they are.

Perhaps the best thing we can do is to say some very plain and practical things about this refined form of hypocrisy.

Take, for example, the custom in many Christian circles of giving "testimonies." Well, why shouldn't one give testimony? "Out of the abundance of the heart the mouth speaks." Why shouldn't a person be allowed to tell the story of what Jesus

Christ the Savior has done for him? The old story of how he went on for years with no peace in his life, bound by secret servitudes and chains, and then how Christ became too strong to resist and finally brought him to the peace of his Cross and the joy of forgiveness. I know many people who have been conquered and converted by such a testimony, when no sermon had ever accomplished it before. Did not the apostles do the same thing? Testimony is really a genuine form of proclamation.

But yet there is always this fact that we can observe in ourselves and in others. In many of these testimonies, especially when they take the form of constantly repeated stories of conversion, a record played over and over again, the focus somehow gets shifted. The testimony no longer deals with the Lord who has acted upon us, but deals with the level on which this action took place, and this level is ourselves—we who play a very interesting role in it. We really mean in all this to give praise to our Lord (*soli Deo gloria!*), but in reality it has become a bit of autobiographical pomposity. We make an impression with it, and this pleases us; so we go on repeating it frequently. But everything that contributes to the glory of the person and hence takes the glory away from God becomes a lie. Thus in the end it turns out to be a false, oversimplified black and white statement.

So it made no small impression upon me one time when an old servant of God, after listening to another who never stopped telling the story of his repentance and conversion, poured a little water into the wine of his pious testimony by saying, "Come, come, Peterkin, put the cork on it or it will lose its bouquet"; in other words, it will lose the fine fragrance which it has only in secret quietness with God.

This is exactly what Jesus meant, exactly what one might call the double-tracked, self-contradictory character of our life. True, we worship God by means of our words, we give testimony. But in reality we have already falsified the theme, be-

cause we talk about ourselves. And this is just what fixes our
secret intent upon men, the people whom we want to impress.
This is the terrible contradiction in which we often involve ourselves and for which we should stop and examine ourselves
thoroughly and in all objective earnestness.

Therefore every Christian who wants to confess his Lord—
and certainly every one of us, and by no means only the preachers, desires and is committed to do this—must again and again
enter into solitude with God, into the quietness of prayer, where
no man listens to what is said. Only the words that come out
of this quiet conversation with the Father, this secret place,
can really magnify our Lord and bring him close to a man.
Everything I talk about with men I must first have talked about
with my Father. And Jesus himself was able to talk to men with
such power and authority only because he sought out the time
and the privacy to talk with the Father beyond all self-conceit
and all pious purposes.

How many people there are who do not find God because
they are this kind of hypocrite, because this false note and this
false perspective creeps into their search for God—even their
search for *God!* How many there are who will not go through
with this wrestling for the truth, for God, for the foundations
of life! They are so bent upon being Faustian God-seekers that
they never really want to reach the goal. One recognizes them
by their mania for carrying on religious and philosophical discussions, for letting their intellect and the earnestness of their
searching shine. And down underneath, to them the peace of
God for which they appear to be searching is much too "simple"
a thing to give them enough occasion to show it off.

This type, which is especially widespread among the intellectuals, is exactly the type of hypocrite described by Jesus; he
is the type of "man in contradiction." The whole theme of his
inner struggle appears to be God, appears to be peace; but in
truth he himself is the theme. He likes the pose of a seeker, he

enjoys his Faustian coquetry. He gathers treasures in a show-window and gets a narcissistic pleasure from them. This is why such a person cannot find peace. He is one of the trials of the pastor, the hardest to deal with and only the miracle of the Holy Spirit can really touch him.

For the Father sees the hidden places of the heart. Here and only here must one begin to become a Christian. Rather curse outwardly and create the impression of carelessness than fall victim to the passion for putting on a show and be caught in the toils of self-conceit. Vanity in one's own eyes is always much worse than vanity before others. The person who fancies himself cutting a "tragic" figure is hermetically sealing himself off from the realm of the Holy Spirit.

If only our hidden life with God is in order and there is within us a secret place of prayer and spiritual discipline and struggle! By this secret stillness and by this alone will God calculate the value and consequence of our life when the hour of reckoning and recompense comes.

So we have said that the message of our text is by no means concerned only with fasting, but rather that it is a call to the struggle of faith. Because we have a mighty Lord, his enemies also exert themselves mightily. Everything within us masses together in the struggle to displace him and possess our heart: the roaring of our passions that prevents us from hearing; the lack of time that keeps us from talking with the Father; the worries and cares that kill all prayer because they pitch us into restlessness and faithlessness; the vanity and the coquetry that rob us of solitude and seduce us into self-importance and thus make God unimportant.

A full stomach or an empty one is a factor here too. Well-fed people often forget that they have no peace and that something vital is lacking. And the rich who have everything are always thought of in the New Testament as being in the greatest jeopardy. But the hunger, which so many of us have learned to know, is certainly not in itself a spiritual discipline and it does not bring us any closer to the heavenly home. Rather the opposite; for usually it brings in its train despair, dullness, care, and weariness of prayer.

But remember this; there is nothing in life—neither fullness nor hunger, neither culture nor rubbled ruins, neither home nor far country—that cannot become a vehicle of infinite grace when it comes to those who love God. For then it is quite simply a question of taking as literally and realistically as possible the promise that "everything works for good with those who love God." The distress we all are having to endure now, the worry about what will happen to Germany, the anxiety for the future of our deeply confused world, the need for food and clothing, and all the other little afflictions are all primarily a question addressed to us. And the question is whether we are going to let all these things lead to sadness, despair, and despondency, *or* whether for once we are simply going to make the tremendous and yet so simple venture of blindly trusting these words of the Lord that they will work together for our good—and that they will do this the *very* moment we dare to fear these things less than we love God.

In other words, the opposite of fear is not courage (courage is only repressed fear). The opposite of fear is love toward him who has overcome the world and who therefore also takes away the fear that prevails in the world. The very troubles with which the devil stokes up our despair can also become the material from which the Holy Spirit forms our faith. So I dare to ask: Who is given a greater chance to experience the miracle of faith, the security of the Father's house, and the unspeakable solicitude of our God than those who come with empty hands and then find them filled by God, those who hunger and thirst and then see and taste that God never allows them to pray in vain for daily bread, that he feeds the birds of the air and even more his dearly purchased children? So let us be watchful and sober and really keep our eyes on him who cares for the birds and the lilies *and* his children (let us do this in the sense of the spiritual discipline and training we have been talking about), in order that these eyes of ours may not be lost in the dark, but keep looking for the hand of the Father.

Then, too, let us also put the cares and the worries, the anxiety and the hunger of hearts and bodies in the hand of him who can change all things, who can turn water into wine, despair into faith, and the fear of the far country into the blessed peace of the children of God.

10

Overcoming Anxiety

"Do not lay up for yourselves treasures on earth, where moth and rust consume and where thieves break in and steal, but lay up for yourselves treasures in heaven, where neither moth nor rust consumes and where thieves do not break in and steal. For where your treasure is, there will your heart be also.

"The eye is the lamp of the body. So, if your eye is sound, your whole body will be full of light; but if your eye is not sound, your whole body will be full of darkness. If then the light in you is darkness, how great is the darkness!

"No man can serve two masters; for either he will hate the one and love the other, or he will be devoted to the one and despise the other. You cannot serve God and mammon.

"Therefore I tell you, do not be anxious about your life, what you shall eat or what you shall drink, nor about your body, what you shall put on. Is not life more than food, and the body more than clothing? Look at the birds of the air; they neither sow nor reap nor gather into barns, and yet your heavenly Father feeds them. Are you not of more value than they? And which of you by being anxious can add one cubit to his span of life? And why are you anxious about clothing? Consider the lilies of the field, how they grow; they neither toil nor spin; yet I tell you, even Solomon in all his glory was not arrayed like one of these. But if God so clothes the grass of the field, which today is alive and tomorrow is thrown into the oven, will he not much more clothe you, O men of little faith? Therefore do not be anxious, saying, 'What shall we eat?' or 'What shall we drink?' or 'What shall we wear?' For the Gentiles seek all these things; and your heavenly Father knows that you need them all. But seek first his kingdom and his righteousness, and all these things shall be yours as well.

"Therefore do not be anxious about tomorrow for tomorrow will be anxious for itself. Let the day's own trouble be sufficient for the day."   *—Matthew 6:19-34*

I

All the idyllic pictures in this text of carefree birds and happy lilies and the glory and splendor of Solomon cannot hide from us the fact that Jesus is saying something tremendously upsetting here; upsetting simply because now it all has to be transposed from the light of nature into drab gray of our every-day life. And it is this very question, whether such a trans-position from the one to the other is possible, that turns our "lovely" text into a hard morsel to swallow. For, after all, our everyday life is filled with some very downright, realistic cares which simply cannot be conjured away. The businessman tor-ments himself with the problem of filling his shelves with goods and emptying them again. In times of competition he fears the transiency of fortune and anxiously he contemplates the coming of reverses. The mother worries about the future of her chil-dren and young people are afraid they will miss something life has to offer. The student worries over his examinations and the aging woman fears that soon the door will be closed upon her.

Is there any need to go on describing this vicious circle of care in which we are caught, this serpent which is constantly biting its own tail? Well, I do not believe that we have come together here for this purpose, merely to listen to this old song that buzzes in our ears every day sung once more in church.

But the question is, have we come together to do the *opposite?* To forget for a moment the tormenting, gnawing, wearing world? To forget the worries we have about the tensions be-tween the East and the West? To forget for a while what may become of that sick husband, that child who is having difficulties in growing up? Well, we are not going to wallow in such questions either. But we do ask whether we have come here to forget, merely to give ourselves a few breaths of narcosis in the religious world removed from everyday concerns and indulge in a little romantic nature study by contemplating the birds of the air and their obviously happier existence.

But if we are doing this, we certainly are missing the point of this Word of God. For the very purpose of this Word is to get down *into* our cares and our fears; its very intent is to encourage and cheer us by telling us that he who said these words about the lilies and the birds bore in his own body all the pains and fears, all the torments and mortal struggles, not because he wanted to soar above them for a while, but rather because he wanted to be in them as our brother and therefore suffer them with us. How then can we so wrongfully use this Word as a drug to make us forget, a means of pious ecstasy?

But just because this is true, the text is so difficult for us. How in the world can the life of carefree birds be transposed into our troubled world? In the face of the brutal problems of existence what can we do with these words: "Look at the birds, consider the lilies"? We fear the reactionary dreams about the good old times because they may cause us to miss the present. But we also fear the romanticism of nature because it can become a flight from reality and therefore dishonest.

Nevertheless I think we must stop and listen when *this* man, whose life on earth was anything but birdlike and lilylike, points us to the carefreeness of the birds and lilies. Were not the somber shadows of the Cross already looming over this hour of the Sermon on the Mount? Was not Jesus already seeing the "tomorrow" of his own life, the tomorrow which he bids us not to worry about, filling up with dark clouds from which very soon the lightning will flash upon him? And does he not see that through these very words, which he speaks and himself lives by, he is actually attracting this lightning to himself? Do you think he had no presentiment of the dreadfulness of that explosion? No presentiment that very soon would come a "tomorrow" when he would have to beg his Father to let this cup pass from him?

Isn't it true that everything depends upon *who* it is that says these words about the birds and the lilies? A person who sees, as Jesus Christ did, the human and the nonhuman domain of the cosmos pervaded with fissures, menaces, and rebellions against God and throws himself and his whole existence into it, who sees not only the flaming signs of his own downfall but those of the whole world flickering on the horizon, who already knows the hour when the mountains shall cover us and the sun and moon will be darkened—well, I should say that, coming from him, these words about the birds and the lilies and their marvelous freedom from care means something different from what it would if it were spoken by some romantic nature lover and dreamer.

So we ask ourselves quite simply what Jesus meant by "care." Does he mean every kind of care and forethought?

After all, there is the anxious love of mothers; and who does not regard the lines of care and concern on the face of a mother with reverence? Are these really lines of guilt?

And is not "care" inherent in every kind of serious work? After all, I simply *must* give thought, agonizing thought perhaps, to whether I am equal to a task because I have to cope with it, to how I can break it down into stages, the obstacles and resistances I must overcome. Even according to Jesus' *own* statement must not a man who proposes to build a tower sit down and count the cost, and therefore "take thought," "whether he has enough to complete it" (Luke 14:28)? Is he really forbidding the sower to work and thus also to take thought?

We soon find that here we are on the wrong track. For what Jesus means by carefreeness is impossible to find in this direction.

He is really directing our attention to the fact that even with and despite this perfectly justified care we can be unfaithful to God, and that we do this when we take all these tasks and gifts, which we have received from God in the first place, and set them *above* the Giver, and thus give preference to the created things over the Creator. But in the language of the Bible this way of turning things upside down is called—idolatry.

We are anxious, for example, about food and clothing. Don't we know that as God's children we get them from God's hand? After all, *he* creates all life and all that is necessary for life. But often how indifferent we are to this giving hand compared with the gift itself. How typical it is of us: we do not worry about whether we remain in the hands of God or what this hand may do with us; we worry only about the *means* by which God is supposed to help us. I say "supposed," for we have all got it in our heads that we are supposed to be helped in such and such a way. *We* must have food and clothing at *this* time, from *such* and *such* a source, and in *such* and *such* quantity. True, we understand that it is *God* who must help us and that we cannot get along without him (after all, we're not atheists!), so we go ahead and ask him for the sources, the dates, and the necessary quantities. We decide, as it were, what "providence" shall be, what the radius and therefore the program of its action shall be. In other words, God is supposed to help us only by opening *the* door we are looking at and carrying out the program which we have planned for ourselves. To leave to him the way in which he will help us, this seems to us a bit too risky, too presumptuous. That God with all his higher thoughts should have any thoughts about how he will help us, that he should let his help break in "unexpectedly," and therefore *contrary* to all our plans and deliberations, in the form of "surprises," this seems to us to be demanding too much of our trust. And yet again and again we are surprised and shamed when this is exactly what he does, when what we need is provided in the most incredible and punctual way.

And because we cling to the ways and means and our own programs, we also have no joy in our prayers and only half of our heart is in them. For the other half is already dwelling on "tomorrow"; already our mind is wandering. It is considering and calculating whether God will really provide the means we pray for and how we can help ourselves in case he does not intervene. Meanwhile the words of our prayer grow flat and musty. They do not make us fresh and glad, as prayer should, but go limping and fluttering to the ceiling, but certainly not to heaven. So we are torn between faith and doubt, anxiety and trust. And in this state how can we ever talk joyfully with the Father and trustfully commit everything—our cares about clothing, shoes, food, and drink—into his hands? In this state how can we ever venture to keep our own hands folded, which, after all, is the symbolical meaning of the gesture of prayer? In this state we rather tend to let our hands drum nervously on the table or secretly reach for the latch of the door which we are stubbornly convinced is the only one through which God's help can come, the way which our own arrogant and untrusting thoughts have devised and deluded us into believing.

This is where Jesus sees the curse of care—that in care we are always looking to our own ways and not to the goals of God, who has his own ways for us. So the first thing he teaches us is to fix our eyes on this goal: the kingdom of God, everything in which God completely realizes his higher thoughts and therefore where he will be all in all. Once we dare to do this, once we earnestly fix our eyes on God's goal for our world and our life, then in every circumstance we will also be sure that everything else "will be ours as well," that is, that then God will give us abundantly all that we need to gain this goal.

Perhaps we need bread and physical strength for years to come because we shall be needed for long years in his service and to help others to find the kingdom of God. Perhaps we need it too because God still has a long way to train and prepare us, so that perhaps as old men and women, after a thousand faults and follies, we may finally find him.

But perhaps—who really knows?—we also need hunger and nakedness and imprisonment, in order that we may lose our trust in our own strength and learn to understand the blessing of empty hands and physical and spiritual poverty, which really teaches us for the first time to cry out for the riches and the abundance in the Father's hands. Often we do not know what to pray for, often we do not know what we need and what to wish for. Perhaps it may be good for us to be released from imprisonment soon, but perhaps the best thing for me may be to remain longer in this discipline. How many a man has written to me or said to me in retrospect to this dark time in his life, that he was glad for his imprisonment and that he would not have missed a moment of this guidance of God, simply because it had been *God's* guidance.

Looking at it from this point of view we already understand better why our preoccupation with our own way and our own advantage, why this everlasting care and anxiety for both is so foolish and dangerous. We only become more deeply immersed in ourselves and get caught in the vicious circle of delusion, instead of lifting up our heads and looking to the goal of God. Let it be enough then for us to know that God will take care of all the ways that lead to this goal: the money we need and also the illness (or the recovery) we need, will come just when we need them. But we will be blessed by both only if we dare to trust that God has set *his* theme for our life, so that now everything, really everything, must serve to the carrying out of this theme.

But how can we really take anything as coming from the hand of God, if we do not keep this theme in view, if we do not let this one thing needful be our sole and ultimate concern?

The man who shirks this care, this concern lest he lose sight of this goal of God's grace, will then have to worry about everything else—the accident he may have with his car, the next tax declaration, every frown on his boss's face. And conversely, the man who constantly keeps in his heart this *one* concern not to lose contact with the hand of God will be able to allow a sovereign carefreeness to govern everything with which he is then in duty bound to concern himself, simply because he is prepared at any time to let God cancel and throw away his own plans and programs. For he knows that the Father's red pencil is not the terrifying instrument of an evil and incalculable censor, but rather that this is the only way that God can lead us to his royal goal. He knows therefore that every red check is not only a sign of judgment, but rather a sign of grace, erected above our shortsighted and deluded eyes, an assurance that *he* is at work and that he will not allow us to fall victim to our well-meant follies and plans.

All this makes it clear why care is "idolatry." We worship the creaturely bread by which we are satisfied instead of worshiping the Lord who satisfies us in many different ways.

We worship money, the tangible values, and still do not find happiness, because moth and rust consume them. And because we know this very well, we go on gathering more and more, and grow ever more anxious to win the race against the moths and the rust. It is not only "joy" that "wants deep, deep eternity" (Nietzsche), but also anxiety and care go on increasing endlessly. We also worry further that thieves may come and take away what we have accumulated: an inflation or a deflation or the internal revenue. So immediately for him who has lost contact with God, the deserted heaven is peopled with imps and specters. Every cloud fills him with foreboding, for lightning may flash from it. Even the horizon is laden with mysteries that evoke tension and anxiety. One never knows what is behind it and what the morrow may bring. Our world becomes a world of cares and specters, and we begin to understand the terrible image our Germanic ancestors used to describe this danger that comes from the horizon, this primal anxiety of life: the image of the Midgard serpent that encircles the globe and is able to crush our whole world in its dreadful embrace. A world surrounded by the serpent—this is the world that has lost the Father, the world of care.

Whoever keeps his eyes on the "means" by which God can help (whoever relies on the miracle men of history, on parties and reform programs, especially when they end with "isms") is entrusting himself to false gods, and down underneath he knows full well that they will cheat him. What a vicious circle: the man who worries and cares worships false gods, and the false gods plunge him into fresh cares and anxieties.

This whole problem of being free from care is not at all a matter of better balanced technique for living which would be less hard on the nerves, but rather of our getting away from slavery to the false gods. Only if we see this can we comprehend the peace that comes to us with its blessing in Jesus' saying that the treasure we lay up in heaven is safe from thieves and rust. He who invests the treasure of his trust in God's bank is the only one who will never be defrauded—either in this world or the next—because it is safe with him whose heart is faithful and loving, whose eye watches over him, and whose hands are ready to bestow upon him from his eternal abundance all that he needs.

How dreadful it is when a man no longer sees all this, when his eyes become deceivers and he loses all sense of the real proportions of life, and then regards the paltry pennies and miserable crumbs more highly than the hand that bestows them and is eager to bestow upon us infinitely greater blessings and abundance than the pennies and crumbs we worry about.

Only one thing is needful and that is this hand of the Father, which is Jesus Christ himself. When we hold on to that hand we have everything—life and salvation, peace and freedom from care; and then quite incidentally, "in sleep," as that wonderful phrase of Scripture puts it (Ps. 127:2), we are also given what this hand has to give: the pennies and crumbs, the food and drink, shoes and clothing, and everything that we need for life.

And the reverse is also true. He who does *not* have this one and only hand sinks into care and anxiousness, into fear of thieves and moths, and persecution complexes; and then no penny is too paltry and no crumb is too small to lie like an incubus upon his chest, a false god and specter that robs him of his sleep.

The opposite of tormenting care is not the carefreeness of those who are amply and securely provided with all the necessities of life—just ask whether the man in the mansion sleeps more peacefully than the man in the tenement! No, the opposite of care is the peace of God, which I can have when Jesus Christ has taken my hand and put it back in the hand of the Father.

We are not carefree when the sea is calm and the ship of our life glides pleasantly along. But we can be carefree even if the waves rise high, when the Lord sleeps in our ship and we know that it cannot go down, that winds and weather cannot hurt us, because he who can command them in a moment is with us. The one care that should concern us is that we do not throw away our trust in the Lord who would sleep in our ship and is able to walk upon the waves. As soon as we direct our cares to the wrong address, namely, the waves, we are caught in the grip of mortal terror and we sink just as Peter did. False care is not to be combatted with an artificial and forced carefreeness—this would be sterile make-believe and would lead to nothing but an ostrich policy. Care can only be cured by care. Care about many things can be cured only by care about "the one thing needful." This is the homeopathy of divine healing.

But there is one last question that may trouble us. The First Epistle of Peter tells us, "Cast all your anxieties on him."

This would mean that we still may have cares and can bring them to our Lord and Savior. So perhaps we may still come to him with the many little things in our life. For it is true, isn't it, that the greatest part of our cares have nothing to do with the great perspectives of world history, but are mostly trifles? Ought we not then be allowed to bring these things into our prayers? Are we allowed only to say, "Thy will be done"? Does this petition mean that we must pay no attention to our little cares and simply go drifting romantically on?

It need only be expressed in this way and we see at once that it cannot have been meant in that way, for the Lord's Prayer itself teaches us to pray to the Father for daily bread and our small daily rations. The fact is that we can come to the Father with *everything;* and Jesus Christ, who brings us to him, comforted the bereaved mother in her sorrow and care for the future; he helped the poor who knew not how they would survive the next day. Even the matter of drink at a wedding he took seriously. So carefully does he watch and attend to our little cares! And because this is so, we can tell him in our prayers the ways and means we see by which our cares may be relieved. We can tell God where we hope to get our bread so that he may open *this* particular door. We can tell him which people seem to have helpful contacts so that he may move their hearts to help. It would be unnatural not to allow ourselves these prayers for definite ways and means, for these are the very things we worry about, the very things we should cast on God. God certainly does not want us to suppress our cares and never let them out; he wants us to bring them to him openly and freely. After all, this is why we are his children for Jesus' sake. And what earthly father would wish that his child should keep anything from him through shame?

But then, having done this, and having the right to do it, it is time to stress the other petition: "Thy will be done" and

"Not what I will, but what thou wilt." What that petition means would run something like this:

"So, dear Father, I have told thee everything that troubles me; I have told thee the ways in which I think I might be helped, and I have prayed that in thy mercy thou wouldst help in the ways I think it should be done. But now, O Father, I draw a line through it all, forget it all and leave it all behind; now do with me as thou wilt. Thy will be done—not mine. For all the world, with its history, its terrors and enigmas must one day end at thy throne; and thou wilt bring it there, despite the opposition and conceit of man. Let my life too, with all its needs and cares, end at the throne of thy heart. Dear heavenly Father, thou knowest the ways and thou dost wonderfully know how to make them smooth. Thou hast ways above all other ways to put to shame our frets and cares and thou will make even the worst and hardest things work together for good."

The man who has many cares also has the greatest chance of faith, just *because* he has so much to bring to his Lord, just because all this can be transformed into a great trust.

There are *many* needs, but only one thing is *needful;* and if we have this one thing, the rest will come—in sleep. That's the royal promise of God and also the royal experience of all the children of God. "To put to shame our fretting, unexpected will it be." And this "unexpectedness," the surprises of God, this is the end of all our plans and cares. God's work can begin only when we have reached the end of our own tether. O men of little faith, why then are you so fainthearted? Does anything ever happen except God's will?

II

Care is a question addressed to the future in fear and trembling. It is the fearful question of what is going to happen. For the future is full of threatening possibilities. There in the future is the endangered harvest burned by a merciless sun, and thronging problems of world politics; the creaking in the world's foundations seems more and more to be changing into the sound of cracking, and we wait for the moment when this precariously balanced structure will collapse and the savage flames of fresh catastrophe will burst from its windows.

We know what all this can mean: hunger, being driven out of house and home, falling into the cruel hands of men. We know the sight and the sound of homes collapsing in flames, the times that are past all human help. We know this because our own eyes have seen the red blaze and our own ears have heard the sound of crashing, falling, and shrieking.

Is there any wonder, then, that we should be apprehensive that all this may repeat itself or that the old theme of catastrophe may be given further variations? We know the torments of which this world is capable. Is it sinful, then, to have these cares? Is it sinful to have known and experienced dread, to know that everything is "possible"?

I think not, and above all I do not think that this is the way to approach the mystery that Jesus has in mind when he speaks of the *disobedience* and the *sin* of worrying. For all these things we have just mentioned, the experiences that have made us knowing and therefore so anxious about the future—all this lies in the realm of the things that come into our mouth, our eyes, and our ears from the *outside*. And this is the realm—our Lord once said—that does not defile a man (Matt. 15:15 ff.). Only what comes *out* of the heart, from the inside to the outside, defiles us and makes us sinful. In these hearts of ours evil thoughts are constantly rising like bubbles of poisonous marsh gas, and among these evil thoughts are also our cares. So *here* is the source and secret of care; this is where we must look.

Therefore if we want to get rid of our cares, this everlasting anxiety, and all the nervousness connected with it, we dare not try to minimize the distresses of the coming winter and just

be optimistic about the world situation; this would only produce a temporary narcosis which would all too soon be followed
by a sad awakening. No, we must let God give us a new *heart*.
Once this heart is decontaminated, then the poisonous gases
and delusions of anxiety will no longer rise from it.

So if we have to stop and consider for a while this heart of
ours, this desperate and deceitful thing, this reservoir of our
guilt and fear, I am aware that this is no welcome subject. Some
perhaps may think, "Why doesn't he leave all these gloomy
subjects out of his sermon today and talk to us about the golden
streets and crystal streams? We've got enough gloom and fear
around us already."

Ah, but we can talk about our hearts as *Christians*, and suddenly it isn't a gloomy subject at all. For these are the hearts
to which all the promises of God were addressed, the central
promise that they can become places of peace and fearlessness,
because Jesus Christ is present and he has rescued them from
the dark powers. Now we can talk about it as Jesus himself
talked about it in the Sermon on the Mount. The first thing
he said was, "Blessed are you. *Already* you *are* in my care. Now
you can look at the terrible abysses without fear and trembling."
So this heart is mysteriously changed and thus the place of terror
becomes a place of wonder. So this terrible heart can show you
what depths you have been snatched from and how great must
have been the love that moved God to make this wild, unruly
heart his own in Jesus Christ. You may show a man marked
for death his face in a mirror and mortal terror may spring upon
him from the glass when he sees himself in this dreadful dilapida-
tion. But you can show a convalescent a picture of himself
taken in his worst illness and it cannot harm him, for then instead
it can become the occasion for fervent thanksgiving.

In this sense, then, as those who have been called by name
and snatched from the depths of fear and guilt by Jesus Christ,
we shall dare to look into our own anxious, burdened, and self-

tormenting hearts. We look at them in the presence of Jesus Christ; in the presence of peace we see how full of strife and bickering are our thoughts.

But how does care get into our hearts? Faust says this about it:

> Deep in the heart nests Care, a question unbidden
>
> . . . .
>
> Ever with some new mask she hides her face,
> Herself as wife and child, as house and homestead veiling,
> As fire, water, poison, steel;
> Each blow that falls not dost thou feel,
> And what thou ne'er shalt lose, that ever art bewailing.

In these words we all recognize our own natural heart. For here we are told that the anxious spirit does not come into our heart from the outside, that it is not the threatened situation of my family, nor my health, nor the menacing constellations of world affairs that cause us care; for all these troubles could also evoke the *opposite* of care in us; they could serve to make us throw away our trust in human help and in both despair and confidence at once commit ourselves to God's mercy. No, what we are told here is that care comes *out* of our *hearts*. I fear that someone will take a shot at me from the dark; I am afraid of denouncers, or people who are jealous of me, or other wicked men. But the shots never come. I am afraid of short circuits that will set the house on fire; but the lines are intact. I fear that my home will be entered and my children killed; but it never happens and the children are playing happily in the sunshine: "Each blow that falls not dost thou feel, and what thou ne'er shalt lose, that ever art bewailing."

This heart has within it a great store of anxiety, delusion, and discord and then it proceeds to work like a weird motion picture machine that translates this store of anxiety and discord into horrible pictures. Then what happens to me is exactly what happens to the spectator in the movies: I am caught in the illusion that these images are real things coming at me from the screen. I literally live with these people and their fate, and in the same way I live with the fearful chimeras of care as if they were realities. And meanwhile, all this comes from my heart; they are all figments of this heart that is "deceitful above all things and desperately corrupt" (Jer. 17:9).

How does this happen?

Just before Faust uttered these terrible and yet deeply discerning words about care he had cried out in blasphemous self-assertion, "I am the image of the Godhead"; and in the next moment he sold himself to the devil.

This is very important for any understanding of the mystery of care. It means that when a man no longer looks at the world and life from the vantage point of the peace of fellowship with God, then he simply has to look at it the way it looks under the dominion of the devil. Ah, but then there is the *threatened* world: doesn't everything end in death? "Past and pure Naught . . . it is the same as had it never been," says the devil at the death of Faust. In the end the Grim Reaper comes to fetch even the greatest of men. Not a trace of meaning, no sense in life whatsoever, says the devil (for the devil is a nihilist): just look at all the crooks and grafters having a sweet life of it, while the good are left in misery holding the bag! This is the argument with which the devil drove Job almost out of his wits, smiting this good man with one disaster after another and allowing the cheats and scoundrels to prosper. He was trying to persuade him that life is nothing but a jumbled confusion of accident and chance, utterly unfatherly, utterly ungodly. A person is a fool to expect divine justice, a fool if he is so stupid to imagine that good will be rewarded and wickedness punished. Haven't we all known this temptation of Job in our hearts? "Haphazard strikes the lightning"—this the devil whispered into people's hearts on the nights the bombs were falling and they understood him: in dreadful resignation they said, "It's fate," when cathedrals fell in ashes and taverns survived the storm.

This is what the world looks like from the devil's perspective, this is what it looks like "this side of God": a blind game of dice, an aimless journey into the unknown. Mind you, in this world everything, literally everything is possible: you can become a millionaire or a starveling, you can be dead tomorrow because a brick has fallen on your head, or you can become an old man weary of life. You can become a governor or be sent to prison tomorrow, or both at the same time. It is absurd to look for any meaning and sense in all this. In a mixed-up world like this you will have to content yourself with the fact that everything, absolutely everything is "possible."

And for this knowledge that anything is "possible" modern man has coined the term "anxiety of life." Earlier generations were aware of the fear of death, but man today is afraid of life. Not because he is especially cowardly when it comes to war and nights of bombing. On the contrary, he is probably more courageous than former generations and some times even foolhardy. But he is afraid of life. He is afraid of everything that *might* happen in this unpredictable world that is loaded with every conceivable "possibility." He feels so terribly alone as he faces all this. If he knew that Someone is *with* him, indeed, if he knew that Someone sends all these things, terrible as they may be, and if he knew that this Someone had a purpose in all this and that there is love in it somewhere, then he could bear *everything*.

But this is just what he does *not* know. And therefore he is helplessly delivered over to the mad dance of life. *He must fear everything because everything is "possible."* That's why the horrible images loom up in his heart and the projection machine of this anxiety of life throws them vividly upon the screen, and "what he never will lose he must be always bewailing." He must bewail it, just because he *could* lose everything, because everything is "possible" in this world of the devil, which Job suffered down to the bitter dregs.

Don't you see now that in the last analysis it is our unredeemed hearts that are behind our cares and not the dangerous things themselves, not even the bad harvest, not even the conflict between the East and the West? It is the *heart* that pictures the world as full of moths and rust, atom bombs and catastrophes, and is afraid of all the things that are "possible" and could happen in an unpredictable world.

This is where we meet the deepest mysteries of our faith. In Psalm 73 we have set before us the utter predicament of a man who no longer discerns the leadings of God, a man who, like Job, saw the terrible and senseless inversion of reward and punishment and therefore was plunged into care and anxiety in the face of this unpredictable world. Isn't the devil in ultimate control after all? The psalmist was almost at the point of drawing this conclusion. And he forbore doing so only because it would condemn all the children of God and turn their faith into nothing but a satanic delusion. Only this caused him to recoil from this ultimate desperate conclusion.

But simply to recoil is not yet a return to the peace of God. It is only flight from a conclusion too horrible to contemplate. And yet this peace of God arches over the close of this psalm like a reconciling rainbow and the good news of the grace of God and peace with him is heard at the end.

How does the psalmist arrive at this peace in the midst of an unpredictable world? Does he arrive at it, say, by a process of reflection in which he discovers the meaning and suddenly the light dawns on him? Does he reflect and then say, it was "because" God wanted to mature me through suffering; "because" he wanted to test my faith in the midst of this crazy, unpredictable world; he robbed me of my position, my living, my home, my dearest "because . . ."? No; we shall look in vain in the whole psalm for this kind of argument. It is the feverish thinking of the worldly wise, who think they can fathom the meaning of life that grasps for this kind of argument. The psalmist scorns it. He simply says:

"*Nevertheless I am continually with thee.*"

How is this remarkable "nevertheless" to be understood? How can it bring release from the anxiety of life?

If there were *one* point at which I could see that there is a living heart that beats for this world, then my anxiety would be removed with one blow. Then nothing could touch me that had not first passed the censorship of that heart and been declared by that heart to be wholesome and good for me. Then in everything that troubles me, in everything I dread the hidden theme of love is at work, even though *I* am unable to detect it in the confused beat of this disjointed world. Then for me it would simply be enough that all these things come from the heart of God and are meant to lead me back to him.

And this one point at which this tremendous liberating comfort and assurance becomes visible and available to me is Jesus Christ. I have used the illustration of the magnifying glass before. Only if we look through the middle of the glass do we see the object behind more sharply and clearly. The farther we move away from it and the more our eyes are focused on the edges of the glass, the more distorted and unrecognizable the object becomes. And the same is true of the way that Jesus Christ helps us to look at life. Only if we view the mystery of life through him, through the Center of history, does it gain its old clarity; for when we look through him we are looking into the heart of God. But the farther we move away from this Center and allow our eyes to wander to the edges the more distorted, impenetrable and satanic becomes everything that comes into our field of vision. At the margins the anxiety of life prevails. Only at the center, the focus, only in Jesus Christ do I see the Father and what he wills for me. I see him helping those who hunger and thirst and in Jesus Christ I see him becoming himself a man who hungers and thirsts, a prisoner, destitute and naked. Here I see God in his Son allowing to throb and pulsate through his own heart everything that is my own torment and desire: the intoxication of power, the admiration of men, and all the dreadful abysses that yawn in my own life. For in the hour of temptation in the wilderness the Son of God took my own wild heart, with all its temptations, all its drunken passions, all its anxiety, into his own breast. So greatly did he love me! He not only had compassion upon those who sit in darkness and the shadow of death, but himself endured the darkness of satanic powers and himself died our death.

When I see in my Savior Jesus Christ this heart of the Father, this heart that beats for *me* and was wounded *for my sake*, then, of course, I do not know, any more than the pagan or the worrying Faust, whether I shall be alive tomorrow, or whether the atom bomb will lay in dust and ashes the summer landscape that now brings to my lips songs of praise and thanks and joy over the glory of creation. Nor do I know (any more than the pagan or Faust) why my beloved, the riches and the center of my life has vanished in the East, whereas my neighbor's husband comes home and starts the old marital rows all over again. As a *Christian* I do not know the answers to these questions. And yet, mysteriously, the care and the anxiety has been taken away from me, because now I can say Yes, because God in his grace has given me the power of acceptance. Now I no longer look at the future in an attitude of tense defensiveness, filled with anxiety over all the incalculable things that may be brewing there. Rather I accept it, simply because a hand is being extended to me and it is the hand of my Savior.

If that divine hand is there, and if this can only be cause for me to rejoice (for who does not know what a helping hand can mean when he is terribly ill, or when it is dark and he has lost his bearings, or when he is pitched into the depths of sorrow?), why should I not also be willing to accept what is *in* that hand, why should I not joyfully walk the road where this hand leads me? In the last analysis it doesn't matter at all whether I "understand" the meaning of my life in all its strange turnings. Rather everything depends on my keeping contact with that hand, because *then* I can say Yes, *then* I can *accept*.

He gave himself for me and made good for all my debts, and if he could do that, then he has only my best welfare at heart even in the heaviest burdens and the roughest roads and he will allow only what serves to my good to come to me.

The opposite of care is therefore not the kind of optimism that persuades itself that everything is not so bad after all, that things will straighten out somehow. The so-called optimists on principle are generally mere windbags, superficial characters who are not serious or courageous enough to face the realities.

Rather, the opposite of care is *faith*. It is the faith that knows the uncertainty of the future and faces all the enigmas and seemingly meaningless events of life. It simply says, "Nevertheless I am continually with thee."

I beg you to note that faith does not say, "Nevertheless I will remain standing; 'what does not get me down makes me stronger.'" Any lout could say that, if the size of his brain did not prevent him from thinking a philosophical thought. No; faith says, "Perhaps I may fall and often I am helpless, but thou wilt lift me up. My understanding is staggered and utterly confused in the face of the great mass of suffering in the world, but thou dost not forsake me, and therefore I too will hold fast to thy hand. For I know that thy love has its way even in the deepest darkness." This is the sense in which faith is the opposite of care. And this is how the Lord himself expressed it when he said, "Do not fear, only believe" (Mark 5:36).

Once we allow God to give us this trust, then we begin to taste something of the royal freedom of the children of God and, mysteriously, our whole attitude toward the future changes. Our first interest is no longer the question (the frightened, despairing question) whether God will help, but rather that other question (the glad, confident, eagerly curious question) *how* God will help. Pascal once said that it is glorious to ride on a ship in stormy weather when one knows that it cannot go down.

This is the tumultuous joy of the Christian life, its laughter, its humor, and its victorious, overcoming power—this knowledge that now our life is a ship like that, a ship in which Jesus Christ sleeps and that never can go down. I know a genuine Christian who has gone through terrible suffering and great danger and is still going through it. He said to me one time, "Now the spiritual danger in my life is no longer that I count too little on God. No, through countless mercies and the unbelievably punctual ways in which he has helped me through, God has made me almost too bold in the way in which I now let him do the work and simply go along with him. Letting myself be carried along is now a state that could become a spiritual danger to me."

However this may be, this man certainly experienced something of God's care and the carefreeness of his children.

This brings us then to the close and we have only this one question to ask: How can we, quite practically, come to this freedom from care in the presence of Jesus Christ?

Listen to a few very practicable rules given to us by the gospel.

1. The first is that we should not artificially turn away from our cares (by constantly listening to the radio, for example, or running to the movies, or some other kind of busy-work), but rather direct our cares to him who wills to bear and share all our sin and all our suffering and therefore all our cares. Not diversion, but directing our cares. This is what to do. Jesus did not say: Look at the ostrich, how it buries its head in the desert sand and so tries to escape the fear of danger. No, he said: Look at the birds of the air, keep your eyes open, stand up straight and look to the heights where God makes known his grace and care.

2. The second rule is connected with the first. You should not repress your cares but let them out. Nor should you keep

weighing them and asking whether they have been inspired by the devil and have their root in unbelief, or whether they are important enough to bring to your heavenly Father. Did not Jesus show compassionate condescension, meeting even the distress of the housewife when the wine ran out at a wedding, and did he not also take in hand that foolish care of the mother of the sons of Zebedee who wanted to see her sons placed, one at his right hand and one at his left hand, in the kingdom of God? Why should not he who forgives our sins smile at our foolishness—smile in *kindness*, rather than be angry with us? Why should not he who loves us common people also love the common little things about us? Why should he not take us as we are, with all our manly energy and our childish fears, our heroism and our petty, often foolish cares, and wrap us round with his compassion? After all, it was his compassion that drove him to leave the glories of heaven and come to us. So, because he is our brother and companion, let us talk with God "as beloved children approach their dear father."

3. We dare not remain alone for one moment with our cares and anxieties; not for a minute of the worrisome night must we allow them to claim our heart. And very practically this means that as soon as our cares appear they must be transformed into prayer. They are highly explosive and if we keep them in our hands too long they will tear us to pieces. And when we see the careworn, tormented faces of people on the subways and streets we realize with horror that these are mangled corpses of people who kept these grenades of care in their hands instead of flinging them away and casting their care on him who in his immeasurable goodness has promised to care for us and whose heart is proof against these perilous things.

But when we turn our cares into prayers a real "transformation" takes place, as with *everything* we bring to Jesus Christ. For then they bring us far closer to the heart of the Father than when we have no cares. He that cares much is also much loved, and he who has many tears to dry feels the gentle hand of God far more than others. The fact is that, in order to be comforted by God "as one whom his mother comforts," one must become a child, with all a child's fears and helplessness and terror of the dark. And this child is still within even the strongest man. He who never dares to cry out "Abba! Father!" never learns that the child within him is crying out for redemption, and instead of finding the royal peace of the children of God, he is left alone with his own artificially forced show of so-called bravery. Conversely, he who immediately and daily transforms every care into a prayer will still have to face the riddles of life and its mysterious leadings. But the riddles will no longer torment him, because he has contact with the Father's heart, the heart he sees in his brother Jesus Christ, that heart in which all the inscrutable mysteries of life prove to be mysteries of love and therefore become consolations and joys. "Nevertheless I am continually with thee."

This is not merely a kind of stubborn, stone-faced loyalty to God, but rather an expression of that joy and happiness I feel when I know that the dark future and the meaningless dice game of life can no longer hurt me, that it cannot faze or daunt me, that in all the storms of life I have a place of peace where I can lay my head and relax and sleep, just as Jesus slept in the plunging ship while the faithless disciples were driven half mad by fear.

4. The whole history of the world with its terrors and uncertainties must one day end at God's throne, even though once more the terrible tides of tribulation, tanks, and atom bombs should sweep down upon us—who knows what could happen? But even *that* will not be able to thwart God's plans and ultimate goal; even *that* terror and travail would only bring us nearer to the goal.

But at the end, across the bloody fields, across the smoldering earth and the all-consuming floods will sound the praise of God,

raised by all the angels, the redeemed, and all who have overcome, because Jesus Christ is Victor.

*At the evening of the world the victory of God will be
celebrated!*

And therefore the last rule against care is this: whenever fear
of the immediate future, of hunger and cold, war and death
become too much for you, then for a moment stop your crying
and pleading. Then in the midst of the storm dare to praise God,
as the disciples in prison praised him. For to praise God means
to see the world from the point of view of its end, of the great
victory of God. And in this praise of God our views of things,
darkened and constricted by the press of battle will be refreshed
and gain direction and perspective.

Perhaps the greatest gift we have as Christians, who know
that our Lord has won the victory, is that even here and now,
not only at the end, we can praise God, simply because we know
what the end will be, simply because we know that there is one
victorious, shining theme that runs through all the loneliness and
homelessness, all the hunger, thirst, and mysteries of this life,
and that is: Nearer, my God, to thee.

He who knows that at the end is God's peace not merely *cries*
from the depths; he also can *sing praise* from the depths. But
then, he who praises God is not afraid.

11

The Judge Accused

"Judge not, that you be not judged. For with the judgment you pronounce you will be judged, and the measure you give will be the measure you get. Why do you see the speck that is in your brother's eye, but do not notice the log that is in your own eye? Or how can you say to your brother, 'Let me take the speck out of your eye,' when there is the log in your own eye? You hypocrite, first take the log out of your own eye, and then you will see clearly to take the speck out of your brother's eye.

"Do not give dogs what is holy; and do not throw your pearls before swine, lest they trample them underfoot and turn to attack you."   *—Matthew 7:1-6*

We live in a time of constant and seemingly never ending judgments.* The columns of our newspapers are filled with reports of accounts being settled everywhere: those who were responsible for the reign of terror that lies behind us are being summoned to judgment. Statesmen, industrialists, leading physicians are being tried. People talk about the collective guilt, or at any rate the collective liability of the whole nation. Individual professions, the rank and file, the educated are asked about their

---

* The following comments refer to the numerous criminal and denazification trials in the period immediately following the war. In recalling them here we do so because they seem to represent an unusually conspicuous eruption of "judgmental spirit" that is present in the world and to that extent have symptomatic significance.

147

part in the world catastrophe. The soldiers are accused of fighting under the wrong flag. Every one of us is both questioner and questioned at the same time. There are constant ups and downs and tos and fros in the courtrooms of our world, an everlasting alternation between the bench and the dock. The world has become a house of judgment. And it will probably continue to remain so. Only with disquietude dare one imagine the fierce mutual recrimination and judgment that will break out when the longed for hour comes when the separated parts of our country are reunited.

What is the ultimate motive behind this passion of judgment, cross-examination, and accusation with which the world seems to be literally loaded? What lies behind the sworn assertions of innocence and the equally solemn self-incriminations and confessions of guilt? What lies behind this fate of our world which has become a house of judgment, surrounding us all with grim, gray walls?

I believe it is simply this: we all sense that our world has gone out of joint at its *innermost* core (and therefore not merely politically, economically, and culturally), that a deep rift runs through the structure of the world. It is no longer possible to live peacefully in this house for it threatens to collapse. Therefore we must seek with all our strength to find out how the rift got there and whose mad wickedness it was that undermined the foundations. Behind this frantic search for the guilty is also the knowledge that we are threatened, that an outrage has been committed and we will find no rest until it has been uncovered and the guilt expiated.

The situation is like that of Greek tragedy: the city is oppressed by the presence of the Sphinx and everyone knows that a crime has been committed and must be atoned for. The accounts must be settled if we are to go on living. The mushroom cloud of Hiroshima hangs like a dark cloud over our world, and if we do not have done with our judging the executions will begin, and the head of the whole world—including all judges, all the accused, and the executioner himself—is in some mysterious way already laid upon the block. This dark premonition lies behind this passionate rage for judging.

So the judgments buzz about our ears, uttered by excited judges, excited because they themselves are threatened, and our voices and verdicts are among them.

One verdict runs like this: "People have been playing a criminal game with power and therefore—say the judges—we must build the new world 'democratically,' that is, in such a way that power will be properly distributed and thus the wickedness of excessive power will be checked."

But immediately we hear the opposite judgment: "Just look at the democracies! It may be that in the democracies the state does not function as a wielder of power and brutal egoism, but in place of that you have a system of group egoisms, interested economic associations, political parties, and other ideological powers." And the conflict of judgments, the furious succession of the judging and the accused goes on.

Another verdict says this: "The cause of our misery is that the dignity of man has been lost, that we have given up *humanity*. So the inevitable result has been the enslavement of whole peoples, the liquidation of the insane, the persecution of the Jews. Therefore the violators of human dignity must be condemned and there must be a new evaluation of the meaning of humanity."

But here again the counter argument is raised, this time perhaps by Christians: "You *cannot* regain the concept of humanity, no matter how earnestly you try, for you have lost God. Only he who takes God seriously can take man seriously; so it is only empty rhetoric to talk about restoring the image of man. It is impossible for you to do this. The fault is that the whole world is in flight from God and you humanists are right in the midst of these refugees from God. If it depended on you, the image of man would dissolve into an unsubstantial shadow. So even against your will, you are contributing to the widening of the rift in the world's structure."

So even on this subject the judging that goes on in the world does not cease. The accusations keep surging back and forth.

Even on the streets the trials and judgments go on. People see German girls in the employ of the occupation powers, rouged, dressed, and marcelled according to a different taste and with strange-looking faces. The judge within us begins to struggle with human contempt and is tempted to hiss cynically, "Shame!"

But again the opposite judgment comes into play and puts us in the dock; for the girls reply, "Don't you see the tremendous excess of women over men; don't you see that we are afraid we are going to miss out? Don't you see that we are doomed to hopelessness because the men who would have been our husbands are lying dead on the battlefields? Don't you understand that we too yearn for fulfillment, that we too would like to have a little of the carefreeness and fun and a few of the pretty things that you older people enjoyed? Who puts us in this situation? We accuse those who murdered our happiness; we are not criminals, we are victims; so stop condemning us when we look for a little happiness in these miserable times, a happiness which you had yourself and which you cheated us out of."

In all this judging, then, *who* should listen to *whom?* Who is to blame, the murderer or the murdered? A terrible uncertainty has come over the world since it has become a house of judgment. We face the utter bankruptcy of judgment: "Judge not, that you be not judged!" And God knows we are beginning to understand something of the wretchedness of judging. We begin to see with a horrible clarity that human censure and judgment can never right the wrong but only increases it. It immediately and automatically evokes a counterjudgment. It is subject to the terrible law of retaliation.

Why is it, then, that this curse that Jesus unmistakably points to here rests upon all human judgments?

All human judgment always has a touch of egoism. When I judge I put myself above the other person and imagine that I am better than he. This is the secret pharisaism that dwells by nature in the judge. In judging I elevate myself and seek to put the other person down. And therefore the judgment never helps him, but only embitters and hardens him. He often feels—when it comes to this natural form of judging—that he is being subjected not to justice but rather to the egoism and self-confidence of the one who is judging. It is no wonder, then, that some downright brutal forms of judgment are hidden behind human judgments.

So we prick up our ears when Jesus speaks of the curse of judging. We sense that this saying is a redeeming and liberating message in the judgment-house world in which we live.

And we should be lacking in common sense if the following doubt did not occur to us. It is true, we reflect, that there is a curse upon judging; but is not the *opposite* of judgment, is not "consistent mercy" equally impossible? Can the world really be ruled with forgiveness and love, instead of the hard law of retribution and punishment? Would not this lead to frightful laxity, to the breakdown of all order, and then would not evil be unbridled and uncontrollable? Should we counsel the allied powers not to condemn the Third Reich and tell them to point out the log in their own eye? Should we turn around and ourselves start judging pharisaically, telling them that they have "no right" to condemn us and that they have reason enough to let mercy be accounted for justice?

In our study of Jesus' sayings concerning loving one's enemies we have already been confronted with the same kind of question. And we saw that it would be a complete misunderstanding of what our Lord said to interpret his prohibition of judgment as a license for laxity and indecision. Jesus calls evil evil and good good, and he is utterly radical about it. Could there be any sharper condemnation than his reference to the swine before whom one should not cast his pearls, or his division of men into sheep and goats? We should be going in a completely wrong direction if we were to interpret Jesus' call to mercy "sentimentally." Jesus is by no means speaking here against the jurists, judges, and public prosecutors. He is not speaking against the stern law of legal order or legal sanctions. He is concerned about something else altogether.

He is opposing human judgment in every case in which we attempt to anticipate the final judgment of God and thus forget that every one of us (from the Nuremberg court, to lowest magistrate's hearing) is on his way to the Last Judgment. That is to say, when we forget that one day all of us must stand before the judgment seat of God, when we imagine that we ourselves are sitting in unimpeachable majesty on that judgment seat, then there comes into our judging the tone of self-righteousness and presumption. Then we are forgetting the log in our own eye. Then the person who is being condemned immediately feels that he should not be treated in this way. Then he knows that the judge has no right to sit on his high horse, in other words, that it is not "just" for him to speak to us from that level. He therefore becomes embittered and resists. He feels that he is at the mercy of a judge who no longer recognizes that he himself is a sinful man in need of forgiveness, who is no longer in ultimate solidarity with him, the accused; but rather feels that he is facing the hypocritical madness of some voice from heaven.

So again and again it happens that the old Nazis, for example, are simply hardened in their attitude, instead of being led to the conversion which is so urgently needed. All too often, and unfortunately all too often rightly, they sense that those who point the finger of judgment at them, or even those who have to judge them because it is their vocation to do so, manifest so precious little realization that *every one* of us, including the professional judge, is under judgment, that we have *all* made compromises, kept silent, and all have a terrible log in our own eye. They cannot help becoming embittered when now the finger of judgment is pointed at them even by those who were prevented from going along with the enthusiasm and vitality of that disastrous movement only by their own laziness, small-mindedness, and lack of spirit (and therefore not at all because they were determined to obey God more than men).

And it is precisely *this* kind of judging that our Lord forbids us, this judging as if we were sitting on God's throne, where no man dares to sit, but before which every man must appear. He who dares to say, "I have no sin," or even *acts* as if this were so, is claiming that he is carrying out God's ultimate judgment; then he is practicing idolatry and is only driving the rift deeper into the world's foundations.

But then what good are all these statements to us? What good to us is the Savior's saying that this blasphemous judging is loaded with a curse? What good is this when every day we see the house of judgment becoming more and more a madhouse and thus a monstrous illustration of the very thing that Jesus was talking about? What good is all this to us when we do not even know how to get away from it in our own small selves? For it is certainly true that this is where it has to begin. There is no getting around it, for it is written on every page of the Bible: all the evil in the world comes out of my heart, *my* apostasy, *my* disobedience. So first things have to be set straight here, at this tiny little point in the great wide world.

Then our very simple, practical question is this: Does Jesus have something helpful to say on this constructive side of the problem at this *crucial* point? And not only something to say; does he have something to give, which only he can give and with which he drives a breach into the dark wall of judgment and leads us out into the open where we can breathe the fresh air of God's world again?

To catch something of this healing power in the words of the Savior listen to the second verse: "For with the judgment you pronounce you will be judged, and the measure you give will be the measure you get."

What a terrible threat that is! For who can stand if he himself is subjected to the unmerciful standards that he applies to his neighbors?

But we must stop and listen to this saying of the Savior as it sounds coming from *his* mouth. We must listen to it remembering that it is *he*, and not somebody else, who is saying it to us; remembering that he who is saying this to us is he who came to us in the name of forgiveness and not of judgment, he who in great love shed his blood for us. Then suddenly there rises up behind the terrible threat a totally different saying, which we see emerging like a lovely kernel from the dark shell, and then what it says is the exact opposite of the threat—"for with the judgment by which you *are* judged you too should judge and the measure you *are* given should also be the measure you give." Surely we know the measure by which we are measured; it is the measure of mercy, the measure of infinite compassion, the measure of the sacrifice that was made for us on the Cross. We are the debtors (exactly as in the parable!), to whom everything has been given, even though the judgment must demand and did demand payment down to the last penny (Matt. 18:21-35). And what these words mean, then, is that we must not be unmerciful servants who mount the high horse over against their neighbor after they themselves have just been lifted out of the mire.

Once we understand *who* it is that is uttering this prohibition of judgment, and that on his lips it is far more than a legalistic prohibition, that it points to the fact that we ourselves (you and I!) have been spared the judgment and are nothing less than pardoned sinners, then the Lord's threat ("the measure you give will be the measure you get") takes on an even more dreadful meaning. For then what it means is this: if you go on judging others, despite the fact that I your Savior bring forgiveness to you, then you are placing yourselves outside of my grace and outside the consequences that this has for your own relationship to your neighbor. Then you are simply putting yourself back on the level of calculation and retribution, and therefore you yourself will be the first victim of your attitude. If you want judgment despite all the grace of God, then ask for it; you can have it. But when it comes back at you and hits you yourself, then do not come back and say, "That's not the way I meant it and wanted it; I wanted it to apply only to my neighbor." Don't you see that your neighbor (the person who has wronged you, who censures you pharisaically,) is also called to accept the forgiveness of the Cross, that I died for him too?

Then how can the blessing which you refuse him be given to *you?* You can determine the level on which you are going to stand, the level of judgment or of grace; and whichever you choose will decide how you are going to deal with your neighbor (not your Platonic assurances about whether you take a Christian point of view or have some sympathy for the church). And this level which you have chosen and which reveals itself in your relationship to your neighbor will also determine how God approaches you, whether as the judge, who puts you to silence, or as the Crucified, to whom you may cry, "Have mercy upon me."

Hence we should be completely misunderstanding the Lord if we were to interpret what he says against the spirit of judgment as meaning that now we must choke down, suppress, and repress every such thought that rises up in us. Jesus has no desire to make moralists out of us. He is not interested in our becoming people whose hearts are full of malicious thoughts but who assiduously train themselves not to let them come out and become acts. This leads only to hypocrisy and self-poisoning. For evil thoughts which are merely repressed go on rumbling about in the heart, poisoning the imagination and troubling one's dreams. Besides, Jesus would not have needed to die for this kind of moral training. After all, his purpose was not to help us to achieve repression; he wanted to deliver, redeem, and liberate us.

So when we catch ourselves judging a girl for running around in the way we referred to we should remember that God grieves for this girl and that Jesus was thinking of her too when he cried, "It is finished." And if we have an associate who keeps deviling us because he grudges us our position and success, and we are tempted to become cynical, we ought to stop right there and ask ourselves what dark thoughts would rise in *our* minds if *we* were in this situation, the black impulses of jealousy and hate that we know are in our own hearts; and that Jesus nevertheless has called us to himself and bestowed his mercy upon us. Then quite of itself (and I know what I am talking about) it turns out that I do not even *need* to fight with my urge to judge; for it is conquered by a higher hand. Then quite of itself, quite spontaneously, there flows from my heart a stream of compassion. And there you have a miracle, like the miracle God performed when Moses smote the hard rock where none suspected there was saving water and the rock opened and the bubbling, springing wonder occurred. I need only open my own heart, this hard rock, to the stream of divine love and compassion and quite of itself it will flow on in a thousand rivulets; not because my own heart has suddenly acquired such peculiar virtues (it remains a wicked and desperate thing), but because this divine stream has great power; it seeks to flow through my heart and out of it again to others, and all the evil spirits of judgment and vexation must be drowned in it every day.

Then, too, there is something else that is taken care of "quite of itself," and that is that this compassion will not degenerate into something merely soft and lax in the sense of that stupid maxim, "To understand all is to pardon all." Who could have greater understanding than the omniscient God? Did he pardon all *because* he understood everything so well, because he knew the motives and the background of the deed?

The writer of Psalm 139, for one, did not hold this opinion. He drew quite the opposite conclusion. He says—and it is obvious that he says it with every sign of horror—that it is a terrible thing to face the fact God knows my every thought and word and deed, that he "understands" all these things. The psalmist in any case does not say: *Because* thou understandest all, thou wilt also pardon all. What he says is just the opposite: *Because* thou understandest all, therefore thou pursuest me; therefore there is nothing I can hide from thee, there is no darkness where thy judgment does not find me out.

No, we are not to pardon all because we understand all. This would not be doing a favor to that demoralized girl or that resentful associate of yours. I might rather talk to them face to face, I might perhaps rebuke them and tell them off. But the point is that I would do this altogether differently from before. Now I would censure and judge them out of *compassion* and the other person would know that I was doing this as one who has himself stood under judgment without the slightest shred of a defense and escaped it only because of God's grace and Christ's cross, and therefore stands on the same level with him, in the solidarity of the condemned and pardoned, and *therefore* as one who has a helpful, positive, liberating message to speak to him.

In this mad world of judgment and recrimination the helpful message can be proclaimed only by those who do not sit on the judgment seat of God, only by those who themselves stand before that judgment, who have broken down before it, but then have suddenly seen in the lineaments of the Judge the face of the Father of their Savior, Jesus Christ.

The truth is that in the discipleship of his Lord a Christian grows ever more compassionate, because he learns to know his own heart ever more deeply and because under the power of for-

giveness he also grows ever more free and courageous to see himself as he is without any illusions about himself. And therefore,
because he has seen the log in his own eye and gotten rid of it,
he may attempt to take the speck out of his neighbor's eye. This
takes sensitive and compassionate hands. And it also requires that
one should have oneself experienced the pain and the relief that
comes when a foreign body is removed from this most sensitive
organ. Only those who have themselves been wounded can bind
up wounds. Only those who have themselves experienced forgiveness bear healing powers in this world. They bring their
brethren out of the evil, suffocating air of the judgment hall
into the out-of-doors where one can breathe and where God's sun
shines upon the evil and the good. And only when a man has
begun to breathe this new atmosphere does he begin to realize
what a dreadful thing it is, not only to be everlastingly judged
and accused, but also to be driven by the constant compulsion
to judge and criticize, constantly to be subject to the desperate
need to hold on to the mane of one's high horse, so as not to fall
off and let people see what a miserable creature one is after all.

And this leads us to one last subtle point in this abundant text.
Here in Jesus' words the fault is described as a log or a speck
and this obviously means that it is a "foreign body," that something has invaded man's most sensitive organ. He who cannot
distinguish between the organ itself and that which is foreign in
it is not a skillful doctor or pastor of souls.

But look: this is the way that Jesus always looked upon people.
When he met the harlot, the publican, the wretch, and also
the possessed and the mentally ill, this is what he knew: this is
not at all the real man, the person as he came from God's fatherly
hand; something alien has entered into him and I must distinguish between the fundamental reality and the alien thing in him.
For him even the worst of men was not corrupt through and
through, but rather a child of God who had been overtaken by

something alien to himself and whose disfiguring moral sores were to be attributed to a "foreign body" within him. Therefore all of these healings are actually "expulsions," exorcisms, as is most clearly evident in the stories of the demon-possessed. They are separations of the real from the alien; they are operations in which a "foreign body" is removed.

And as soon as the sick and guilty felt Jesus' eyes looking upon them in *this* way they began to grow well. There was something special about his eyes. This is not meant sentimentally at all, but very realistically. The point is that they sensed at once that Jesus saw the "real" person within them, that he was not subject to the optical illusion to which we men are always succumbing. We look at people as if they were one big "speck," not seeing the "eye" at all; whereas Jesus saw first and foremost the eye, saw the child who had gone wrong. And because the publicans, the harlots, and the possessed saw this and realized: "Jesus Christ sees *us*, he sees the real person in us, he sees that we are *children*, that we are loved, that God *cares* for *us*"—they grew well. Nobody had ever looked at them in that way before.

When we become disciples of Jesus our eye is changed too. It changes not only in the sense that the log is removed but also in the sense that now it sees different *things* and sides of these things that it never saw before. Now it no longer sees only the speck in the other's eye but the eye itself, in which God created his royal image. It sees not only the harlot in the girl—the speck —but rather the mourned, unhappy child. It sees not only the venomous schemer in the bad associate or denouncer, but rather the human being who is called to live in the royal freedom of a child of God but prefers to live in the slavery of his hatred; it sees the one who has been bought with the price of blood and is in danger of losing his costliness.

The man who is given this gift of sight stops judging because he has been blessed with seeing something else than the speck. And he sees the miracles of God's love that would flourish everywhere if only *we* were not forcibly preventing them by our unmercifulness and our judging spirit.

A Christian is a person who sets out to discover children of God and then finds them everywhere. True, he too will see the *specks*, for love makes one sharp-sighted; it notes the smallest changes in the one it loves. But love, which has itself gone through the saving operation, discovers the speck in order to *help* remove it with gentle hand; it does *not* discover the speck in order to exult and forget the log in its own eye.

Jesus Christ makes all things *new*, not only our hearts but also our eyes. The world quite literally looks different for those who see it in *this* light. And it not only *looks* different, it *becomes* different. Through atom bombs it is merely held in check, but secretly the abysses are opening up within it. Through the renewal of hearts and eyes, however, it is redeemed and renewed. We have our life by virtue of this miracle. And we must hold still for God that this miracle may happen in us and thus let the healing powers of our Redeemer flow into this dark and fevered world.

12

An Elementary Course in Faith

"Ask, and it will be given you; seek, and you will find; knock, and it will be opened to you. For every one who asks receives, and he who seeks finds, and to him who knocks it will be opened. Or what man of you, if his son asks him for a loaf, will give him a stone? Or if he asks for a fish, will give him a serpent? If you then, who are evil, know how to give good gifts to your children, how much more will your Father who is in heaven give good things to those who ask him? So whatever you wish that men would do to you, do so to them; for this is the law and the prophets."

—Matthew 7:7-12

A person must surely be dull of mind and hard of heart if he does not catch the fresh breeze of realism that blows upon us from the first verse of this text.

It simply and tersely tells us that we should ask, seek, and knock. If we do this, we are assured in these brief, lapidary terms, that certain things will happen: what is asked will be given, what is sought will be found, the door on which we knock will be opened. And what it says is: now *do* this, just try it!

In other words, when there is a wish to come into contact with God, a wish to gain "peace," or even to catch a hint that somebody there on the other end of the line is listening to me and is interested in me—all this is not a matter of instituting some great thought processes. It is not a matter of deliberating, for example, the arguments for and against there being somebody there who rules the world and has a heart for me. Nor is it a matter of *feeling*, of being in a prayerful mood or of being at some special turning point in my life, such as welcoming back from imprisonment the person I love most or receiving notice of his death. It is not a matter of being deeply moved by a concert or the touching good-night prayer of a little child that puts me into a devout mood for prayer. Nothing at all comes from such considerations, and these feelings trickle away in the sober reality of the next hour.

No, this is rather a matter of *doing* something, of our being presented with a clearly defined and utterly simple task, namely, to ask, to seek, and to knock.

When we face a great task, let us say, the establishment of a business, the writing of a book, or the beginning of a course of study, we may easily be overwhelmed by faintheartedness; for suddenly all the problems that will have to be mastered seem to concentrate at one point. Then the questions arise: where am I going to get space and facilities for the business, where can I secure sufficient working capital; and if I do get hold of all these things, who knows whether it will succeed anyhow? After all, in a time of chaos and crisis like this, my own energy and initiative is the smallest factor. Other factors may enter in, changed currency situations may upset all my calculations, and the whole world situation may change.

When I stop to think of all these things my initiative may well shrivel into a heap of misery and discouragement.

The exact same thing can happen when I approach the very great task of straightening out my relationship to God. I really want to do this, for I am so restless and dissatisfied; my life has no center; my work, even when it is successful, seems to me to be a threshing of empty straw; there is no blessing, no grace, and therefore no joy. So for this reason, if for no other, I want to straighten out the foundation of my life, gain contact with the Father, find peace in the midst of rush and restlessness.

But then all the *difficulties* that stand in the way loom up before my eyes. Will I be able to stick out this Christian life? Will I be able to muster up the self-discipline to set aside each day the necessary time and concentration to talk with God and listen to him? Will I not be able to manage and manipulate more easily a lot of things in my life if I do *not* have to face the eyes of divine majesty every day? Would it not be easier simply to follow my own fragile conscience which is always inclined to be lenient and can always be brought around to agree to dubious enterprises? And then the main thing, is the real and ultimate *assumption* correct at all? Does God exist at all? May it not be that all the religious hardships I have taken on in my life are based upon sand and illusions and therefore have been done for nothing at all?

We all know what such thoughts are and how discouraging they can be. And now it is just as if Jesus had caught us in the midst of such anxious thoughts; for right from the start he gives us the effective remedy for them.

What he is saying is that when you are facing a task that is too big for you, the best thing to do is to divide it into small sections or stages of work; then at once the whole thing will look different. It is just this kind of division of labor that he is talking about here. *Your* task, says Jesus, is to ask, seek, and knock. *God's* task is to answer, let himself be found, and open the door. So you simply have no cause to worry at all. You do not need to be nervous about whether God really has the *power*, whether he really *knows* your need, whether your petition has really reached his *ear*. God has guaranteed all this. This should not and need not be your worry.

Indeed, we could reduce the gospel to this brief formula: *it teaches us everything we do not need to worry about!* We need not worry about whether we shall be saved. We need not worry

about whether we gain peace. We need not worry about knowing what is coming, about whether some way out of this utterly
hopeless looking political situation of ours will be found. None
of this is our concern; all this has been taken care of ever since
it pleased God to become our brother in Jesus Christ and to
share our destiny in suffering, dying, and rising again. From
now to the end of days this Jesus Christ wills to slumber and
be with us in our little ship as the waves run high. It is simply
not our concern whether *we* survive the waves and reach the
Last Day. This is all taken care of by him who slumbers in our
ship and in whose hand the ocean is but a quiet pool.

So, too, it is not ours to find out all the theoretical answers
to the problem of prayer; ours is simply to *ask*. This is not
something to be pondered, but *practiced*. With Jesus we are
always sent immediately to work. And as we do the work, as
we pray, we learn what it is all about. It is exactly the same
as an experiment that we have to make: you must try prayer and
then try it again and again.

Jesus, of course, is not speaking of this experiment of prayer
as would a researcher who is making this experiment for the
first time, a scientist, for example, who is experimenting with
atomic destruction for the first time and does not know how
it will turn out, since the laws of nature involved here are still
to be revealed in the experiment. Jesus is rather speaking of
the experiment of prayer as a teacher who has already performed
the experiment a hundred times, who not only knows the natural
laws of the kingdom of God which are at work in it, but, as it
were, sees them from the inside and therefore knows very well
how it will turn out. That is to say, it will turn out that he who
asks will receive abundantly and that to him who knocks the
heavy door of divine mysteries will open.

In all this, of course, one dare not forget the person who is
uttering these words. For all these laws hold good only on this
one assumption, that Jesus Christ be present. Not only because

he said it and because he is an authority dare we risk the experiment of prayer, but really because he is present. Who is he, then? Well, on one occasion he called himself the way to the Father and on another occasion he said he was the door to the fellowship and thus to the Father. So there is a way to the Father, and life is not merely a pathless jungle of creeping vines, nightmare sounds, strange voices, and anxious dread. So—in him —there is a door, and not merely the great black wall of hopelessness against which we are constantly running. *And because, and only because, this way and this door is there, is prayer possible.* And therefore prayer is always made—consciously or unconsciously—in the name of Jesus. And therefore even the idea of experiment finally cancels itself out. For an experiment is always a carefully considered, methodically pursued question addressed to nature, in which the answer may confirm but may also negate my expectations. But here the answer is there before the question is asked, the way is there before the search begins, the door is there before the knocking starts.

In Jesus Christ everything is already bestowed upon you: the peace, the answer, the blessedness, the fellowship with the Father. Now it depends only on your discovering it, or better, on your accepting it, on your not quitting, but availing yourself of the way and using the door. All the rest is none of your concern. Everything *has* been taken care of, and you may be sure, by the very fact that you have begun, that you have already been found. And therefore you can *joyfully* seek and resolutely knock, for unless you do this there can be no opening of the door.

But I already suspect what you are going to say to this. You will say, and you will in fact be expressing an experience which is shared by pagans and the disciples of Jesus alike, "Haven't we all knocked hundreds of times? Everybody has tried to pray at some time or other, even the mockers, the skeptics, and the atheists. But never did we hear anybody saying 'Come in.' There was nothing but terrible silence and I heard nothing. Why, then, should anybody go on knocking? Why should these people who stand in the subway stations, whose faces are so weary and empty, go on knocking? Even those who are gathered here this morning, do any of them really go on knocking? We have 'heard' that silence behind the door so often that we know very well what happens: nothing. We heard nothing but our own breathing and our own words."

We mentioned before what Rilke said in one of his letters about this telephone called Jesus in which people are always calling "Hello, who is there?" and nobody answers.

But I ask you, when we do this have we really lifted the receiver and dialed the right number? Or have we merely dialed *ourselves?* For then, of course, we hear only a hum.

This means, in other words, that we dial ourselves when in our prayers we think only of ourselves, only of the things we want, the bread, the promotion, the return of our missing son, the shortage of goods we need so badly, and thus do *not* think of who it is we intend to speak with here, and that properly we should leave the ways and means to his boundless mercy, his omnipotence, and his higher wisdom. But when this happens our prayer cannot break away from the spell of self-concern, then it never gets beyond the ceiling, then we hear only the derisive humming, but never those relieving, cheering words, "Here I am, my child."

So this knocking and calling is a very peculiar and special thing. But there are not only people who have stopped knocking because they did it wrongly and therefore never heard the words "Come in!"; there are also other people who hold the firm opinion that there is no need for such a thing as knocking. These are the so-called religious people. In order, for example, to experience God in nature or in a Beethoven symphony, of course I do not need to knock on the door or do anything else of the kind. All I have to do is to leap into the fullness of God, because it is everywhere, in every tree, in every sparkling wave, in every mountain glow, in every measure of the immortal music. "Like a rushing through primitive mountains" this religious person (says Rilke in the letter referred to above) breaks through to the one God who so generously allows us to speak with him every morning, *without* any need for this "telephone called Christ," and we might add, without any need for knocking first or entering a door.

I mention this not because I want for the moment to talk to those outside these windows and criticize the outsiders. No, I do so because this look outside the windows (which is really a look at our own selves) gives us a real lead to the special meaning of what Jesus says here about "knocking." For, after all, knocking at the door is a sign of respect. It indicates that I do not have the right simply to "walk in," that I do not have the same rights here that I have in my own home, where I can go in and come out as I please without knocking. For when I have to knock before I enter, say at the door of an office or someone else's home, this is where another person's castle, another person's territory or sovereignty begins; here I dare not simply walk in; I must stop and knock first.

And this is precisely what is meant by this reference to knocking in our text. You cannot have access to God quite so cheaply as nature, where all I have to do is walk in. It is by no means a foregone conclusion that I may enter. For God is holy and I should be consumed beneath his gaze if I were to enter into his presence with unclean lips and unclean hands (and what have they not said and done!). But the fact that I can enter, the fact that I need not be consumed in his presence, the fact that I can sit at table with him as a friend and honored guest—all this I owe to him who opened the door for me and is himself the way to God's presence.

This, surely, is just the opposite of any kind of natural, self-evident access to God. It is a miracle, the miracle of God's good heart. It is the miracle of that love that gave its only begotten Son and shed his blood for us. And the fact that I must first stop and knock before I go in is a reminder of this miracle. For he who waits within is not merely the "dear, kind God," but the holy, living Majesty, who had to allow his most beloved to be torn from his heart in order that I might be drawn to that heart and taste his peace. The fact that I must first knock reminds me of the distance that separates me from the holy God, of all the suffering, the shed blood, and the Cross that had to be endured that I might have this access, that now makes it possible for me to enter and share the joy and fulfillment of the Father.

So knocking on the door is a sign of the miracle: the miracle that there is a door, that there is One who *is* the door, and that I may enter and speak with the Father.

There are certain doors, especially in government offices, that have on them a sign that says, "Enter, do not knock." If you enter, you usually find yourself in an empty anteroom or an unoccupied corridor. So there is nobody there who sets any value on his privacy. And this brings us again to the so-called religious person, within ourselves and in others, who does not recognize the zone of divine majesty, but simply strolls about in his noncommittal religious freedom. This is the kind of person who indulges in a bit of religious thrill over a lovely sunset, or enjoys —quite incidentally and without ever committing himself as a believer—the prickling thrill of witnessing a mass or some other ritual act; he may even have some appreciation of sacred places and the *St. Matthew Passion*. But he passes through them ultimately untouched. He has discovered a vogue word for this "not knocking," a word frequently used by the so-called existentialists and the intellectuals in the big cities: "I am my freedom," says Orestes in Sartre's famous play *The Flies*. What this means is this: "I do not need to knock; the world belongs to me and not to God. The world is *my* game preserve, nobody can touch me, punish me, command me, or limit me."

But this "free man," who regards every door as being marked "Enter, do not knock," pays a price for this nonchalance, this arrogant charging through every door. He pays for his usurpation of the whole world, not only in that he plunges into the catastrophe of the utterly uninhibited and brutal superman (and we know from our own bitter experience what that means), but he also pays for it in that he can no longer find the *real*, the *right* door, and is doomed to go wandering about in empty anterooms and bleak, dark corridors where nobody is to be found. Here he enjoys his freedom, a freedom which is so dreadful because it exists only in this icy no man's land. He is banished to a strangling solitariness in which he no longer has contact with anyone or anything. This is the ghastly hallmark of a humanity that no longer knocks, that no longer knows a door behind which someone is waiting for us.

And it is no accident that this same philosophy of existentialism, that lives by this slogan "Enter, do not knock," also possesses a dreadful key word by which it describes the fundamental feeling that characterizes this fatherless man wandering through the dark corridors; it is the word "anxiety."

In the world we have anxiety—this is the only saying of Jesus people still repeat. We have anxiety, because he who overcame the world is no longer with us. But this last clause is no longer repeated; it has been forgotten.

I think we Christians should have more compassion upon our fellow human beings who live in such fear of the world and at the same time rave about their freedom. We should intercede for them with the Father far oftener and far more fervently, since we are so fortunate as to know the door that opens day by day as we knock upon it, giving us access to joy and peace with him. Is it not like waking from a sad dark dream to be told that there is a door at which we may knock and that someone is waiting for us there? Is it then really a restraint upon

our freedom that we must stop before we enter the door and
not merely walk in? Is it a restraint that then we are really
received as children and friends and can be "at home" in the
house of the Father? Is it really a curb upon us that there we
are under the eye and the discipline of the Father, giving obedience to him? Is this restraint? Or is it not rather the glorious
freedom of the children of God that we should be permitted to
do this? That someone is there who sacrificed and suffered all
things for us and now expects that we shall not throw away
this dearly purchased dignity? That someone is there who takes
away from us the fear and the loneliness of those dark, endless
corridors and brings us into the festal hall of Christian life and
peace?

Is there any greater joy than this—that we may knock and it
will be opened to us and that there is someone there waiting
for you and for me? Is there any greater joy than this—that this
should simply be true?

But the door that opens to us and beyond which we find the
Father does not merely lead us into a secluded room where
nothing goes on except beatific conversation and devout delight.
The end of all this is not merely that state that lovers seek where
two can be alone and away from the world.

No, here at once we are put to work again. Here too there is
something to do, something to be put into practice; for there
can be no relationship with the Father that does not also include
a relationship with our neighbor. A prayer that does not include
my neighbor and brother (the nihilistic fellow, for example, who
no longer knocks and must wander through the dark corridors)
is not a prayer. And a service of worship which is not at the
same time a service to my brethren is not service of God, but
merely opium and pious titillation. Then God has no desire to
hear the solemn phrases of such prayers, the droning sound of
even the great Reformation hymns, and the recitation of even
the most correct sermons. So it cannot be otherwise; the vision

of our neighbor must immediately appear before us: "Whatever you wish that men would do to you, do so to them."

Perhaps now you may think: Well, there's nothing so special
about that. You do not need this Jesus of Nazareth to know this
commandment and to act according to it. Isn't this merely saying what all of us know by nature: "What you do not want
others to do to you, do not do to them"?

But I should like to ask you this: Do not Jesus' words about
our neighbor mean something altogether different? Something
that one can understand only if again one keeps strictly in mind
who it is that is saying this, in other words, only if one sees in
every word of the Sermon on the Mount the preacher of it?

That is to say, what I wish from other people and should then
apply to them too (namely, this love, this regard for them as
persons, this acceptance of them as neighbors) is the very thing
that is given its deepest stamp by what was done to me by Jesus
Christ. Here a heart turns in love toward me, though I lift up
my hand against him. Here one loves me, though I am not worth
loving. Here one regards me with honor, though I am dust and
ashes, a nobody, before him. Here I am bought with a great
price, though I have frittered away my dignity. And ever since
that happened to me I know that a man can live only because he
is loved, only because the great miracle has happened that made
God become his Father. Nothing else deserves to be called life.
It is nothing but lost motion and dreary desolation, a paltry,
piteous wandering through dark corridors. When a man has
forgotten that he is the apple of God's eye, that he is loved and
purchased at great price, his life loses its infinite value. Then
he asks only how men can be used, whether they contribute anything to society, whether they represent productive labor forces
or not. And when they no longer have this utility, they are
thrown on the scrap heap, liquidated, abandoned to hunger.

All that we have experienced in this respect in our own midst
and all that we hear from our brethren beyond the Iron Curtain

is an illustration of this utter self-degradation of the man who no longer knows that he is loved and therefore has lost the meaning and value of his life.

Only he who knows that his neighbor is the apple of God's eye really respects his inviolability. He who forgets this violates his neighbor and merely turns him into fair game. And the dreadful catastrophe of humanity today is nothing less than a sign that we no longer see our fellow human beings under the love of God and its holy protection.

"Whatever you wish that men should do to you, do so to them."

Do we know now what men should do to us? Do we know what we should do to our brothers? Everything that we wish for ourselves and also should do to our brothers can only be a reflection and a passing on of what we have received from Jesus Christ. What did we receive from him? We learned that there is One whose fatherly heart is open to us and that, no matter what happens, we are his beloved children. We learned that we are not orphans, left lonely and forlorn in this brutal world, but that we have a home, our Father's house, where we can knock on the door and know that we will be received with rejoicing like the son who came back from the far country.

But all this was accomplished by *him* who does not leave us desolate, but will abide with us, our way, our door, our brother, our companion.

To him be glory, praise, and thanksgiving!

13

Venturing the Harder Road

"Enter by the narrow gate; for the gate is wide and the way is easy, that leads to destruction, and those who enter by it are many. For the gate is narrow and the way is hard, that leads to life, and those who find it are few." —*Matthew 7:13-14*

Since the collapse of our country at the end of the war it has so happened that I have talked with many people with widely differing views of life, ages, and professions concerning the real cause of our collapse. Uniformly, the conversation moved toward the ultimate questions of life itself. For I did not find a single serious-minded person who did not feel obliged to look for the ultimate causes of the repeated world catastrophes and collapses in very deep-seated crises, indeed, in the so-called religious crises of modern man, or at least to surmise that part of the cause lay here. The universal diagnosis was that mankind had thrown off all bonds of religious awe and now was not happy with its freedom but was beginning more and more to find it a curse.

In most of these conversations, however, an astonishing and rather alarming fact becomes evident, and that is that so-called Christianity is in danger of becoming a fad among us and that people think that it is possible by means of a large-scale re-Christianization to create a broad basis, a "wide and easy" *way*, by which it is hoped that progress may be made. "Christian" politics, "Christian" social order, "Christian" morality—these might be the forces and structures that could cope with the breakdown of honesty in tax returns, the breakdown of marriage, the moral decay among our young people. All this might provide a foundation—or better, a "broad way"—on which we could make headway and expect a great new departure.

But this flight into Christianity, this resort to the ideology of the Christian West, in other words, this attempt to lay out a "broad Christian way," is a highly dubious thing. For it has nothing whatsoever to do with repentance and renewal and therefore has nothing at all to do with the very thing which is of central and decisive importance in the message of Jesus. It is rather merely a form of religious panic. It is well, therefore, for us to note right from the beginning that the "wide" way of which our parable speaks is by no means merely the road where gross sinners lurk, a highway inhabited by thieves, adulterers, denunciators, and sluggards, but that the broad way can also be staked out with road signs bearing Bible passages and words like "eternity," "God," and "Christianity."

The conversations on these questions took pretty much the same form. Thus, for example, in the discussion that followed an address I made in a certain city concerning the German catastrophe a young, very earnest and active businessman said something like this (I quote it as representative of many others):

"It is a good thing for once to have been able to hear a 'theologian' speak about the causes of the collapse and the present misery in the world. For, after all, the general breakdown in the realm of morals, the breaking of international treaties, the general uncertainty in the face of political threats, the rage for power, imperialism—all this is due to the fact that statesmen, nations, and individuals have ceased to respect the divine order. This is why in my business I can no longer depend on my people as my father and grandfather could. Everybody simply grabs at whatever seems to give him an advantage at the moment. Brutal self-interest is the order of the day. And anybody who does not believe this has only to take a look at the battle that goes on in an overcrowded streetcar. Therefore our world will never find peace until we again respect the ultimate sacred values and laws. But only Christianity can help us to do this. That is why I have gone back to the church, even though personally, I do not know much about its doctrines. But I recognize Christian morality, the ideals of reverence and love; these are the only things that can help us. Therefore we must go back to the 'Christian West.' "

The fairly mixed audience that listened to all this for the most part nodded their heads in approval. Here was a decent, congenial man. He was really in earnest about it. Undoubtedly he had hit the nail on the head in many respects and they thought it was to his credit that he, who had once left the church, should make this public testimony.

And yet there is something wrong, something disturbing about what he said. In the last analysis what he was saying was this: now that the politicians and scientists have landed us in this cruel wilderness with their modern philosophies, now we'll have to resort to the Christian ideology!

Did not the devil in the hour of temptation *also* offer the Lord Christ the kingdoms of this world? That is to say, did he not propose that Jesus Christ should lend his name, his personality, his teachings as a program for reconstruction and constitution for a great world government? "Your Christianity, Jesus of Nazareth," said the devil, "your Christianity as a political ideology and foundation for a whole culture, an undergirding philosophy for art and science, would provide a broad road on which everybody could travel. After all, you're too good to die on a cross. You've got what it takes to rule the world. You have a program, Jesus of Nazareth. And here I am, offering you the world in which you can realize it."

We know how Jesus replied to this offer of the devil. We

know that this was just what it was to him—an offer of the *devil!*
Could not this devil, who is able to disguise himself as an angel
of light, also be assuming the mask of the serious man who talks
so convincingly and effectively in a discussion of the Christian
West that goes on today?

And the reason why we have the uncomfortable feeling that
there is something not quite right, something fishy about those
words of the young man suddenly became clear when in this
same discussion another young man took the floor and delivered
himself of this passionate outburst:

"The previous speaker is certainly right in saying that all the
mischief is due to the fact that we have broken away from the
eternal foundations. But what good is that conclusion to me,
what good does it do our people and all of us? How can *I*, how
can *you*, how can all of us get back to those foundations? And
that means very practically," he passionately cried out in the
meeting, "how can *I* become a Christian? It is just eyewash to
talk in general terms about Christian points of view and Christian ideals. It doesn't help a single poor soul for me to say to
you, no matter how correct it may be: loyalty, honesty, respect
for law and the dignity of man can thrive only in a world that
has learned again to stand before God, to fear and love him, to
trust him, and to pray to him. But all of this helps me not one
bit, no matter how right it is, if I, personally, cannot believe in
this God. Then I still can't help to lay any Christian foundations. In a month from now I expect to be married; shall I be
married as a Christian merely because I say to myself—and I say
it just as sincerely and certainly as correctly as the previous
speaker—that the general breakdown of marriage and our own
marriage difficulties will be remedied only if we get back to the
religious foundations? Shall I be married as a Christian even
though I cannot believe in this God, cannot believe in him *even
though* I know very well that I *must* believe in him, that *all* of
us must believe in him, if we really want to help our people and

our country? And therefore the real question for me, and I think I speak for my whole searching generation: How can *I* become that kind of a Christian, a *personal* Christian?"

Then he turned to me, the speaker of the evening, and said, "You say that a man can become this only through Christ: 'no one comes to the Father, but by me'—but that's just the trouble, I can't do it. I can't find that narrow gate, I can't find my way through that bottleneck. And therefore all these wonderful insights of the previous speaker about the ultimate causes of our disaster and the so-called religious renewal of our people are of no help to me at all, no matter how correct they may be."

When he had finished speaking I felt like saying to him, "You are not far from the kingdom of God" (Mark 12:34). This is what the Lord Christ once said to another man who likewise had spoken a very true word about love, without suspecting that this love was present in him who was standing there before him and that he must struggle with all his heart and soul to find him.

To be sure, it is not usual for a preacher to repeat such discussions in a sermon, but my concern has been to discover the point at which Jesus' saying about the narrow gate and the easy way speaks to us in *our* time and in *our* situation, the point where it painfully rouses us out of our dreams and illusions, and at the same time speaks to us comfort and promise.

And my conviction is that that young student put his finger on exactly the right spot. It is true that Christianity is in danger of becoming a kind of fad. People think it is necessary and beneficial; they gush about the broad way of a revived Christian West. The dogma of Christ the God-Man is, of course, medieval; you can't expect to establish the broad base of modern humanity on that. There is no power in that any more for leading the broad masses of the people. But what Christianity calls the fear of God, after it is worked over a bit and turned into "religious reverence," this is something we have to revive again. And without the Christian idea of love and humanity it wouldn't work very well.

In what he said this young man made a thoroughly New Testament observation: that without the person of the Savior himself one cannot have this at all; that there is no such thing as a broad road of general convictions that leads us to the Christian ideas of love, humanity, and reverence, no such thing as a broad road on which everybody could somehow walk together and get along with each other, orthodox and freethinkers, pietists and idealists, enlightened intellectuals and conservative citizens, and whoever else might be counted in the Christian West. He observed perfectly correctly that one arrives at these Christian ideas—if we are going to use this horrible term—only when one has come to terms with Jesus Christ, only as one goes through this very narrow gate and down this narrow road, and thus only as one makes a decision, which means, when one does *not* do what the majority do, but rather at the crossroads chooses to take the narrow, lonely path with Jesus of Nazareth.

"I am the way," says that lonely man who died forsaken on the Cross. This must be a very small and narrow thing. "I am the way," say the Christian ideas that attract so many today. "I am the gate," says the politics of Christian culture, says the Christian West, says Christian-colored religiosity. But that may well be an all too broad, an all too smooth, and all too polished road; it might well lead to the abyss.

"No one comes to the Father, but by *me*"—by me, through me, the most lonely and despised of men, the man of sorrows and death, crowned with thorns and spat upon. This is the narrow gate, the narrow way. This is the way, and this is the only way, that I want to point out to the seekers and inquirers in this hour, because this is what the Lord commands.

Well, what does this mean? It means, in the first place, that when Jesus here contrasts the narrow and the broad way he is demanding of us a *decision*. We dare not go on in the same old jog trot of our daily work, in the chase after the paltry pleasures we desire, a bit of love and the movies, a bit of good food and progress in our job. Rather we must have a *goal* in view; we must ask ourselves: What am I really living for and what must I do to inherit eternal life (Mark 10:17)?

Generally we human beings live according to the law of least resistance, that is, we do what the majority does. We live pretty much at random. And here the path of least resistance is called the broad way. All of us are by nature on this road when we go on living in society as such. And right here Jesus startles us by calling us to halt. What matters is to find a very particular *entrance*. And that's not comfortable. And the way that leads to this entrance is uncomfortable and narrow. You simply can't let yourself go wandering anywhere you please, because there is an abyss on either side of the path. By this he means to say that the road of the Christian life is not a simple thing. Often it is much more comfortable not to be a Christian. That way you will get through this world of lies much easier, with fewer obstacles and much less trouble of conscience, for in this world a Christian should be an exception, should live as a shining signal of another kingdom. You will get ahead easier and with fewer scruples in this world of brutality in which the Christian should practice love, in this world of fear in which the Christian should be a source of peace.

And if right from the start you don't want all this, you can't walk this narrow road. At first Jesus is always a resistance to us, always uncomfortable and inconvenient, always something that says "Stop." And if we are not willing to admit this, we falsify him and turn him into that soft, sweet Nazarene we see in the sentimental pictures of him.

But this decision for him and the narrow way means not only a parting from our previous path; it also means the willingness simply to entrust ourselves to him and to let him lead us down some utterly new, adventuresome, and strange roads. This decision also means parting from other *persons*. Jesus once uttered the hard saying that the disciples must be prepared to leave even father and mother; indeed, he was not afraid to use even the word "hate" in this connection (Luke 14:26). And he also said that disciples must also be prepared on their part to *be* hated (Luke 6:22)—otherwise they could not be disciples.

So discipleship means cross-bearing (Mark 8:34), persecution (Matt. 5:10), and derision; and the more seriously we take our discipleship the more we will get of it. The road leads through a thousand deaths, through partings and loneliness, and often we must let even the most beloved persons go, sensing that they grow more distant and strange toward us. The great in the kingdom of God all had to go through blood and tears and terrible loneliness.

So to begin with, Christ is not the one who would win the Christian West and the masses for his ideals, overarching them all like a unifying myth. Indeed, he never has been with the masses and the many; he avoided them and went to the people who were lonely and forsaken in their guilt and their need, the people who really could not help him to win the world and organize propaganda campaigns on a big, broad scale. In the first place at any rate, he stands like a pier in the stream of men and nations, separating the floods and allowing them to surge high and angrily upon it.

And the fact is that every one of us, drops as we are in those waves, must pass by that pier. There is no smooth sailing along in the stream of life since this pier, Jesus Christ, has been erected in the midst of our world. It takes us through decision and separation, through death and loneliness; in any case, it does not flow through the humdrum channel of the crowd.

And through this loneliness all men who have encountered him have had to go. From the beginning the church was the community of solitaries, the community of those who were "called out," of those who first stood in ultimate loneliness before his eyes.

Who were they? Well, there were the people who were invited to the marriage feast (Matt. 22:2-10). They were called away from their fields and oxen, even from newly married wives; they were obliged to leave off from their business, their vocation, everything that filled their minds and imaginations and quite simply break away from it all. Jesus can use them only as they are quite alone. One day in eternity when they stand before God's throne—and, after all, this is the moment for which Jesus wants to prepare them—they *also* will not be able to take all these things with them. There again they will be completely alone.

And there are the people with their illnesses, their leprosy, their blindness, their darkened minds and shattered souls. And with all this they stand quite *alone* before Jesus. (How terribly isolated and lonely is the mentally ill person!) All of us carry our pack alone in ultimate loneliness, even though thousands of others bear the same lot, even though thousands like me are homeless, exiled, orphaned, and uprooted. For every single person experiences and bears and suffers these things in his *own* way and therefore in a totally different way—and therefore—*alone.* So we are alone in our suffering. Every suffering makes a person lonely. And consequently, each one steps out of the crowd and makes his way alone to the Savior, and then too this Savior belongs to him alone.

There are the publicans and sinners, the adulterers and thieves. How lonely their guilt has made them! Sin has such a horrible power to isolate us; you know this and I know it. And so they too stand alone before the eyes of Jesus, and he is there for them, completely available to each and every one, as if he were the *only* lost soul in this whole world.

And finally there are the people with problems, the intellectual and religious problems they drag about with them; Nicodemus, for example, who comes secretly by night; nobody understands him any more. For our inner tensions and questions isolate us too. "My friends don't understand me; my parents don't know the way things are inside of me"—how many a boy, how many a girl, says something like that. And to these solitary individuals too Jesus speaks his helpful word. For them personally and alone, he has time and love and individual concern. And perhaps on the very night the Master was talking with Nicodemus, Judas was thinking to himself, "Ah, why doesn't he sleep instead of squandering his strength on this one individual! Why doesn't he conserve his strength? Why doesn't he sleep and gather strength to make a great speech tomorrow in the market place in Jerusalem? Then we would soon get on with this Christianization of the world. Only that kind of strategic goal is worth the candle for the Messiah." Such may have been Judas Iscariot's thoughts that night, for he thought in large dimensions; and for that very reason did *not* understand the kingdom of God.

And now I have said enough about the narrowness of the way, of the decisions and partings and the loneliness that comes as we stand beneath the eyes of Jesus.

But in talking about all this, have we not made an amazing discovery? As we have heard that this is a hard and narrow way that leads through dying and dark places, have we not suddenly seen in the narrowness the breadth, in the dying the living, and in him, who seems to make living so hard, the great liberator?

All along, then, I have already been preaching the gospel between the lines, for we can never speak about Jesus—even when we have to speak of the narrowness of the way—without constantly speaking of the joy, the comfort, the promise, and the liberation that exists wherever he is.

For, I ask you, what was the experience of these people whom we just mentioned, the people who stood utterly alone before Jesus with their guilt and affliction, standing there, far away from men and things, in that narrow gate through which a man can pass only if he is utterly alone? Was this a moment that depressed and cast them to the ground? Well, the fact is that every one of them went forth from that hour as healed men, as new men with a new future before them. That's answer enough. For we have already seen that, just as I must bear my personal suffering, my personal homelessness, the hopeless cancer in my body, the unhappiness of my marriage—just as I must bear my personal guilt, which nobody else knows about, and bear it all *alone*, with nobody else to help me, so too I can experience the tremendous liberation and absolution of my Savior only as I meet Jesus Christ face to face in lonely, personal encounter.

When the paralytic was brought by his friends and set down before Jesus, wedged in as he was in a crowd of people, at that moment those two, the sick man and the divine physician, were suddenly completely alone, even though the crowd and his closest friends were standing close by. Suddenly Jesus was there for this *one* man alone, as if there were not millions of others in this world. But this one man, this one erring and tormented human being was worth enough to him to command his compassion, to give himself wholly to him alone. And you too must go through this lonely, personal encounter with Jesus. You too must stand and talk with him in this narrow, constricted gate where he meets you, standing there before you alone, where no man and no thing can accompany you.

Perhaps you may ask me, how does one know that he is there, standing before one? How does one know that one is suddenly confronted with the narrow gate—when, after all, he is so invisible and always there lies heavy upon one's soul that terrible, frightening silence in which one feels that there is nothing there, even though one really wants to "experience" his presence?

The answer to that is relatively simple. Anybody who wants to have some inner sensations and revelations and feelings will be disappointed. These will be "added" to him insofar as they are good for him, quite incidentally and unsought. But first the decisive thing has to happen in your life; first you must face him utterly alone and let him be there for you alone.

And in order to arrive at that point, you must forget this whole crowded church. Perhaps it is the sight of this big congregation that is carrying you along, the rapt attention and the mighty, uplifting singing of the hymns. Perhaps you are hiding yourself among all these hundreds of people and letting yourself be carried along on a wave; and under the spell of this gathering it may seem to you that there really may be something to this Lord of the church, the Lord of this congregation, after all. Well, if that's what you think, you are still far from the kingdom of God; for then you are still on the broad way, which does not lead to peace. For, as I have already said, this broad way that leads to the abyss is by no means just the highway of the scoundrels, the sharpers, the swindlers, and the fourflushers. No, that road is wherever people march in a mass and simply trot along with the crowd because everybody else is doing it. And therefore even a church service can become a broad way, if you merely want a thrill, if you want to let yourself be carried along and uplifted in the tingling, exciting atmosphere of the many.

Now, if only *one* word, of all these words addressed to many and heard simultaneously by many, should hit home to you and cause you to say, "This means me and me alone; this touches an abscess in *my* life, which the man up front can't possibly know is there; this touches a secret sin in my life, which keeps me from finding peace and which I cling to so tenaciously that hitherto I have dodged the narrow gate"; or if you are compelled to say, "This is balm poured into *my* wounds, *my* secret misery, *my* secret despair; everybody else can leave here without anything having happened to them, his words may have missed *everybody else;* but *me,* he has struck straight in the heart. . . ."

Only then will Jesus Christ *himself* have spoken to you in these words being uttered here. Then in, with, and under the words of a poor, weak man a bolt of divine lightning will have struck the ground before your feet and suddenly lighted up the dark landscape of your life. And again when a little later we all say the Lord's Prayer together, if you forget the impressive sound of the chorus of many voices, speaking it with you all around you; and if when you say, "Forgive us our trespasses," you mean, not the guilt and wickedness of the whole world, but your own utterly personal sin and guilt—and you know very well what it is that you have to carry through that narrow gate today—then you can be sure that Jesus Christ is there for you, for you alone, and that he is speaking to *you* that sovereign word of pardon: "*Your* sins are forgiven." Do you understand—not the *world's* sins are forgiven, but *yours*, yours alone?

Only in this narrow gate, only in this solitary chamber, only in one solitary niche of this great church can you become a child. Only there can come into being what is called in the language of the church a personal Christian.

You need not think or fear that I am preaching religious individualism. This has nothing to do with an "ism" or any other silly notions that come out of the witches' cauldron of godlessness. For this niche which I just mentioned is in the midst of the great cathedral in which the whole community of the Lord is gathered. Everything you have to leave behind when you face Jesus Christ alone and settle accounts with him, brothers and sisters, your job, your friends, your marriage and your children, is given back to you again, but now in a new and different way.

In other words, one does not find membership in the congregation of Jesus Christ by indulging in a beautiful service of worship, by being impressed perhaps by something said by some brave bishop, or by feeling secure in this environment. All this is nothing but the broad way, nothing but mere trotting along with a crowd. No, you will find entrance to the community of Jesus Christ, a home in the church, security in that place against which the gates of hell cannot prevail only if first you have stood utterly alone before Jesus. Only then will these people in the youth group, the Y.M.C.A., the men's groups and women's groups really become brothers and sisters whom Jesus has bestowed upon you, standing with you in a bond of union that endures beyond death and beyond the Last Day. Previously they were at most good comrades and nice companions.

The law of inertia of the Christian tradition which you have allowed to carry you along, the religious instruction which has stamped you for life, the habit of church-going, which perhaps you will never get away from—all this will help you not at all; this can be overwhelmed in a trice by the gates of hell—it needs only a bit, perhaps of Bolshevism, to blow it to pieces. You can't stake your life and death on that. But once you have stood in the narrow path, where this lonely figure has refused to let you pass him by and has taken everything away from you, then you will receive all these things back again; then it can become a blessing to you. Even your wife, your husband is suddenly a completely different person to you when you go back to him after having been in the narrow gate, even though you were married as a Christian and were given the blessing of the church. Suddenly he is no longer merely the person you love and who is good to you, or, the other way around, the person who has become so terribly estranged from you during imprisonment, so that you hardly know how to begin over again with him and your marriage is endangered. All of a sudden for you he has become the one for whom Jesus died, for whom Jesus lives, for whom he gave up his life in heaven. Suddenly you see him with different eyes. Now your life is filled with new gifts, new tasks, new perspectives. A new person has, as it were, been freshly born and therefore *sees* everything anew. He sees the tensions of the world situation with different eyes, for he knows that East and West, orient and occident are in the hands of him who is at the same time wholly present for you, for you, the poor, the lonely, the guilty. He simply sees the dark, veiled future, with all its paralyzing hopelessness differently. For in its dark clouds there shimmers the dawn of that day when he will come, when all will be fulfilled according to his plans and nothing will be lost.

So we could go on at length, contemplating all that will be given to us afresh and all that we will see with new, liberated, redeemed eyes.

Only he who is prepared to die receives life. Only he who goes through the narrow gate and down the narrow way gains the gift of a new breadth and amplitude, the breadth of the church with its many brothers and sisters. (And what a thrilling thing it is to experience the breadth of this fellowship when you are lost somewhere and suddenly you find disciples, who are bound to you as brothers and sisters!) And the breadth of the world, too, will be bestowed upon you in a new way after you pass through the narrow gate, with all that we love in this world, but also all that is tormenting and depressing in it; for then we have found the One from whose hand comes *everything:* love and sorrow, people whom we need and who need us, gifts and tasks, joy and pain. And we are assured, comforted, and confident because all this comes through his hands, these hands that reach out for us and bless us, as if we were all alone in this world, and yet which hold the oceans and the very globe itself safe and secure in their sovereign grasp.

14

Time's Up!

And some one said to him, "Lord, will those who are saved be few?"
And he said to them, "Strive to enter by the narrow door; for many,
I tell you, will seek to enter and will not be able. When once the
householder has risen up and shut the door, you will begin to stand
outside and to knock at the door, saying 'Lord, open to us.' He will
answer you, 'I do not know where you come from.' Then you will
begin to say, 'We ate and drank in your presence, and you taught
in our streets.' But he will say, 'I tell you, I do not know where you
come from; depart from me, all you workers of iniquity!' "
—*Luke 13:23-27* (*in connection with Matthew 7:13-14*)

In the last sermon we saw that every one of us is summoned
before the face of God alone, and that no one can help us in the
ultimate decision of our life. Just as every one of us must die
his own death, so he must also stand alone before the throne of
God. Only alone can one go through the narrow gate. To be
sure, God then gives us brothers and sisters, we can then live
and breathe in the community of Jesus Christ, and it is an immeasurable gift to be at home everywhere among Christian people. But first one must go through this narrow gate completely
alone; no man can relieve us of this decision. How often we
would like to relieve of his decision a person who is wrestling
over Jesus and yet cannot make up his mind about him, as a
mother would like to take upon herself the pains of her sick
child and would be happy if she could do so.

But there are things in life that simply cannot be delegated, circumstances in which one cannot take the place of another, things that each individual must go through by himself, things in which one can only pray to God that he may graciously help our brother or sister to get through. The new birth is a hard and painful hour in which even those nearest to us must withdraw.

But true as it is that here you and I are called to an utterly personal decision, this picture of the narrow and the broad gate nevertheless has another side.

It also causes us to look *outside* and constrains us to some very serious and somber thoughts, which are especially troublesome for young Christians.

What a miserable minority sets out for church on Sunday when the bells begin to ring, while the rest go on with other affairs! Again, how few of those in this poor, scattered little troop of church people can really say that they live in the peace of God and that Jesus Christ is their one comfort in life and death! May not thoughts like these—croaking, raven, melancholy thoughts—have been going through the mind of that man who approached the Lord and said, "Lord, will those who are saved be few?" He may have seen what was happening on Jesus' preaching journeys: some hung upon his words, devouring him with their eyes; they had been touched. But then they departed and probably by the next day they had completely forgotten it all again. Only a handful remained, but even these dispersed on the eve of Golgotha. And behind those who were listening, he saw the *others* moving down the street: the farmers driving their oxen, the maidens carrying water jugs to the well, the couples flirting, the lads telling jokes, the women chattering, the men talking politics; and all this going on in the very hours and days and years in which the great world upheaval was taking place, in which our destiny for time and eternity was decided.

It was just like today when the Salvation Army sings and

preaches on a street corner; the autos hoot, the trolley cars go clanging down the street, people hurry past, and hardly anybody notices that suddenly the kingdom of God is there in their midst. The traffic officer lifts his arm and "rules the hour"; everybody's eyes are on him. From somewhere comes the chirping sound of a hymn tune, struggling with the waves of sound rolling through the street. Who thinks of him who rules, not only the hours, but all eternity? Who listens to the words in which eternity is present in judgment and in grace?

And from the many who go their various ways behind the little group of listeners, apparently unconcerned with the words and deeds of Jesus, our eyes involuntarily turn to our *own* situation in which we live day by day in this century of the masses.

Has the judgment been pronounced upon these many; has the judgment been pronounced, for example, upon all these people who go streaming in and out of the doors of trade and business? Who can hope to reach their ears and make himself heard at all? Is it all up with them; are they hopelessly lost? And why then have these few devout people been chosen? The thoughts of this man, who is obviously deeply interested in Jesus, weigh heavier and heavier on his mind as he approaches the Lord. But did not Jesus himself aggravate the gravity of these thoughts when he fastened our attention upon that narrow gate, which only a few will enter and—what a fearful picture for us today— at which in the end a great queue of panicky, pushing, jostling people will try to shoulder their way in, just as people crowded into the shelters during the bombing raids when the horrible sirens proclaimed death and destruction upon the housetops? The sirens of the Last Day begin to scream and suddenly they all realize how unprotected and lost, how terribly lost they are. For in the shadow of the Last Day, at the end of all things everything looks so different, so dreadfully different from what it does on our daily walk down the street or from the perspective of an office chair or a turning lathe.

Did we not all have exactly the same experiences, the feeling
that the great stone buildings of our cities, our solidly built
homes—ordinarily the symbols of human security—had suddenly
become horribly uncertain places, places that might suddenly
fall in upon us? And so in the sudden realization that the world
might be lost we push and crowd at the gates of security, and,
behold, they are shut tight. "Lord, if that's the way it is, who
will get in?"—that's the question this man is asking. "Don't you
see the masses of this twentieth century? They are still outside
and nobody is telling them that the sirens are sounding. Is that
the way the plot of world history is to turn out: ninety-nine
per cent lost and one per cent saved? Why then all this expenditure of God's saving activity, in the end it's only a matter of
terrible, unfathomable predestination—if a few have tickets to
get in and all the pushing and searching for entrance is nothing
but a farce for all the rest? Have you no pity for the masses,
Jesus of Nazareth; after all, didn't you die for *all?* If that's the
senseless way that the world's history is going to end, are you
really the one who was to come; or shall we look for another?"

We know what is going through that man's heart and mind,
because it is our own heart and mind.

But strangely enough, Jesus does not answer his anxious question. He simply sets over against the question a command:
"Strive to enter by the narrow door." It is as if he were saying:
You keep worrying and lacerating your heart with a question
that doesn't concern you at all. How the world's history is going
to turn out, how the books are going to be balanced, how many
are going to heaven and how many to hell, this is not your concern; this is hidden in the counsel of God. Brooding and thinking about this only diverts you from the real question, the task
that God has assigned to *you.* For you yourself are the theme.
You strive to enter in!

It is surprising to note the questions to which Jesus does not
give answers, no matter how seriously and sincerely they are

asked. There are questions by means of which people drown
out the real demand that Jesus makes upon them, by which they
evade certain decisions and try to shift the whole program of
Christ on the same innocuous track. So, for example, the silly
question that was asked in Matthew 22:23 ff.: If a woman marries
seven brothers successively, in each case becoming a widow, to
which of the seven will she belong in the resurrection? As if
there were not more sensible and pressing things to worry about
than such questions. Luther once replied to the profound question of what God was doing and how he occupied himself before he created the universe: "He was cutting switches with
which to thrash inquisitive questioners."

This "wrong way of putting the question" appears most
clearly when the disciples wanted to know of Jesus when the
end of the world would come (Matt. 24:3). Jesus did not answer
their question in the sense of giving them the date they wanted,
but again answered with a *command:* Watch, for you know
neither the day nor the hour when the Son of man will come
(Matt. 25:13). Obviously, what he is saying is: this brooding
over the position of the hands on the clock of the world is something that does not concern you. God alone knows when the
midnight hour will come and the mighty clock strikes twelve.
And therefore speculation about this question only leads you
away from the real question and the real task which is assigned
to you, namely, the command to be watchful and to live every
hour in view of the coming Lord. Who knows why the five
foolish virgins ultimately fell asleep? Perhaps it was precisely
because they had talked themselves to sleep discussing when the
bridegroom would come. After a while it is easy to fall asleep
talking about such religious problems; indeed, such discussions
inevitably put one to sleep. And who knows why the foolish
virgins neglected to fill their lamps with oil? Perhaps again because they were discussing this problem and thus forgot the
essential thing. How many there are today who keep musing

and brooding about the "decline of the West" instead of allowing God to strike this wrong way of putting the question out of their minds and letting him make of them new men from whom streams of living water flow into this desert of decline, this wilderness of our decaying civilization and thus become a staying and renewing force in all this.

I would like to shout something into all this paralyzing discussion that goes on every day, all this spellbound preoccupation with the great unknown of the immediate future, the next war, the question of what we shall eat, wherewithal we shall be clothed, and where we shall live.

I would like to cry out in the midst of all this: "He has showed you, O man, what is good; and what does the Lord require of you but to do justice and to love kindness, and to walk humbly with your God?" (Mic. 6:8). Do you understand? You are *told* what the Lord requires of you. You brood about when fresh war, burning, and death will break in upon us. You just wear yourself out with that kind of thing. For we ruin ourselves with all these false questions and fall into a terrible paralysis. Therefore listen: you have been shown what God requires of you, and this means in very practical terms (I am simply applying this word of the prophet to your situation): put your life so in order that tomorrow the great catastrophe may break in upon you. Practice the keeping of that word that says that whether we live or die we are the Lord's. Use the time, which may perhaps be short, to practice love wherever you can, and be a joyful flowing fountain in the midst of the desert of paralysis, hopelessness, and sullen disillusionment. And be humble before your God, by accepting what he sends to you and surrendering your own false and romantic plans for your life to his mysterious fatherly will.

What a *release* it can be from our anxiety, from all this trembling and bleating, all this croaking and nervousness if I am simply given such marching orders as these: you have been told,

O man, what the Lord requires of you; which most certainly does not mean to talk about the "decline of the West" or the date of the Last Day and the great collapse of the world, but rather to go ahead and do a very definite piece of work. You have only to read your daily Bible text to know what your quota for the day is. You need only look at that young war widow who needs your help or that refugee who is having a hard time of it and is yearning for a good word or a helping hand. The first thing Jesus always has to do to us is to cure our habit of asking the wrong questions and our wrong way of looking at things.

And so it is with the narrow gate. It's not our task at all to ponder about who will get in; our task is to walk into it ourselves. All questions that do not issue in action and have nothing to do with the command of God lead us straight into a confused underbrush of problems and drop us there. And so it is with the question of predestination which is evoked in our text: Are only a few predestined to salvation? Jesus simply ignored this question because it brought up a false subject, a subject that is reserved only to God. And therefore he replies "*Agonizesthe*," which means literally: "Struggle in dead earnest to enter in." And "in dead earnest" means to stake your life on it. Venture above all the thing on which your life most depends, your favorite sins, your strongest passions, the thing you least want to give up—and you know very well what they are in your life— even if they be "goods, fame, child, and wife." God can only be known as one is willing to stake one's life. And he who consents to be recruited and mobilized for his kingdom cannot take a furniture van with him; he must leave everything behind and can only have them as if he had them not. All this Jesus meant when he said: strive in dead earnest to enter in.

And then when he goes on to say, "Many will seek to enter and will not be able," he uses another word for this "seeking" which in the original means something like this: there are the people who are moved merely by wistful longing, by mere homesickness, the so-called religious people who would like to have what they call peace: "Sweet peace, come, ah come to my heart." But no battles can be fought with mere longing and a bit of homesickness for the Father's house; you can't break the spell of the far country, you can't bear the Cross with that! And perhaps when the sirens of the Last Day begin to scream it will be these "yearners" who will stand before the narrow gate of the world to come and plead: Did not yearning drive us into the church? Did we not invite you to be our guest at our meals?

And he will say: I do not know you.

So you see, in the presence of Jesus the only way we can approach this dark question of predestination is to listen to this call: struggle in dead earnest, beware of this pious yearning and this religious prattle. The person who wants to peek into the mysteries of God and then jabber about it is precisely *not* the kind of person who is seeking with all his might to enter into God's security, into the door of the Father's house. He is more like a buzzing fly or a butterfly, beating against the lighted windows of the house, not understanding the glass wall that keeps it from the light to which its obscure instincts and creaturely yearning drives it.

Therefore this saying, "Strive in dead earnest" is not only a hard saying; it is also a *liberating* word. Now we know what it all depends upon. Now we know what our goal is. Not that we have to shut our eyes and turn off our thinking machine as we walk God's road and see the many people with empty faces and hopeless eyes. Not that we are forbidden ever to ask the anxious question: "What will become of all these people?" Jesus has no desire that we should be all tied up inside with repressed questions which we are not allowed to ask; he does not wish us to grow stiff-necked because we are constantly having to turn away from the problems that clutch at our hearts. No. All these questions remain. But they are mysteriously transformed. In his presence they become tasks, commands; suddenly they become creative and positive.

We have only to think of what Jesus himself did with these questions. In the garden of Gethsemane was not he, too, shaken by fear of the future and suddenly desolated by the shadow of his cross?

But in that hour did he allow himself to be devoured by the question of how he was going to face it and whether there might be some other way out? Not by any means. Rather he wrestled to find the task that the will of his Father was setting before him, and then at his command he rose up and walked straight into that task. And the moment of obedience was then also the moment of consolation, and there at his side was the angel who went with him.

There are no angels inhabiting our brooding speculations. But never yet has there been a man who rose up in obedience and "strode into his destiny" whom God did not accompany with his consolation. The roads of God down which we ride in obedience, like Dürer's "Knight defying death and the devil," threatened by the specters of dread in our own breast and perils upon perils by the roadside, are flanked on either side by invisible, mysterious guardians.

And then too, did not Jesus himself see these desperate, hopeless masses on the broad road? Did not this question of what would become of them gnaw at his heart too? Did he not speak of the misery of this flock that had no shepherd and was therefore being caught in the brambles and falling victim to the wolves? And is not this basically the same oppressive question that is being asked here, whether only a few will be saved? But if this question is hard and distressing for you and for me, what must it have been for *him*, who was on his way to give his life and his blood for all of these people (I John 2:2)? Were all these to perish miserably in their sins, ignorant of this grievous sacrifice made for their sake, while in the Father's house the gaily lighted halls were waiting and the utmost price had been paid for their happy homecoming?

But Jesus' gaze did not dwell in sadness upon this glittering procession of misery on the broad way. No, he himself went out and took his stand on that road, crying out to the crowd to stop and turn around. He laid his hand upon the sufferers, by this token showing the others who saw it that they too were secretly sick, that they too were not well and whole. He forgave sins and by that token showed us all that we are estranged from God. And finally he allowed himself to be run down and crushed by the masses, because the world and its broad ways did not understand him, even though it belongs to him.

He was incapable of contemplating the misery of the multitude without immediately instituting countermeasures and helping them: he sent out his disciples like sheep among wolves. This can only mean a tremendous sacrifice for an utterly hopeless missionary task! For, once we begin to think about it, wasn't it a monstrous thing to send sheep two by two into a pack of wolves? But is there a single thought, a single statement or calculation in the New Testament that indicates the hopelessness of this undertaking? Is there a single hint that shows they were asking: Will the wolves be influenced in the slightest by the sacrifice and service of these defenseless ones; will they simply turn back to their howling and bestial games as if nothing had happened? Will the world take any notice whatsoever of the sacrifices of the servants of the Word and the blood of the martyrs? Will this change the world one single bit? Indeed, *has* it changed at all? And if only a few will enter the narrow gate anyhow, why all this effort and expenditure, why all the blood and tears, why the Cross?

But, strangely enough, not a word is said of all this. On the contrary, they went out and obeyed, and as they went and obeyed they were comforted, and in this very obedience they made the most wonderful discoveries. They discovered that the powers of darkness retreated before their preaching of the Word (Luke 10:17), they experienced the joy of serving, the joy of finding one lost soul for whom the angels in heaven rejoiced; and that was reward enough for all the toil.

How different everything looks, depending upon what attitude you take toward Jesus' words. Whether, for example, you try to assess critically what can possibly come of Jesus' saving work; whether the whole thing is a hopeless affair; whether this message still has enough vitality in it to turn this age of the masses around, and therefore whether it would not be better for you simply to sidestep this dangerous expedition into the realm of the wolves. *Or* whether you take his word and go out and do what he has commanded and begin right now to practice love, to give the Word to your neighbors, and be an oasis in this wilderness world!

But when you do that, how different everything becomes! What encouragements, surprises, and miracles await him who acts in obedience instead of standing back and anxiously appraising, who entrusts himself to him who promises to be our rod and staff in the dark valleys and will be with us always, to the end of the world.

So in the discipleship of Jesus everything is transformed. Cares are transformed into prayers, and therefore into something that no longer drags us down but lifts us up to the peace of God and thus makes us free and positive. Paralyzing thoughts become an active obedience that gives content and meaning to our life. And on the rough roads and narrow paths the angels wait for us. In the dark valleys sounds the voice of the Good Shepherd, and in the desert flow the springs of eternity which are the consolation of God. Instead of "craven thought and anxious vacillation" there streams the joy that is promised to all who serve in the name of Jesus.

Why is it that there is such liberation from anxious thoughts

in this command "Strive to enter"? Is Jesus sending us off to
an unknown goal, merely telling us what Goethe said, "Who e'er
aspiring, struggles on, for him there is salvation"? This would
be a very vague and uncertain thing, and the New Testament
makes it clear to us that it is not the struggle and the striving
itself that counts, but rather that one must respect the ground
and goal and motive of the struggle. "An athlete is not crowned
unless he competes according to the rules" (II Tim. 2:5). The
striving "in itself" can become a mere mercenary pursuit, and
the aspiring struggle may be a mere adventure motivated by
the romantic idea that God delights in these gladiators of life
and ultimately approves of these stormy rebels and activists,
regardless of what they strive and struggle for. No, the consolation, the new and positive thing lies in Jesus because he says to
us: you do not strive just for the sake of striving, but because
that narrow gate is there, really open to you and offered to you.
Just as surely as I, Jesus of Nazareth, am among you, proclaim-
ing this message, so surely am I myself this gate and this way.

Do you understand, then, that what is here commanded in this
imperative, "Strive to enter," is at the same time *offered* to you,
given to you, and is fulfilled in him who is here speaking to you?

You perhaps may be among those who hear Jesus' words like
a distant bell and are moved by the sound of it, but still do not
know where it is or even whether its ringing is meant for *you*.
How many there are who say, openly or indirectly, those melancholy words of Faust, "The words I hear full well; but, alas,
it's faith I lack." And what is that but to say: I'd like to live
in that world in which my mother once taught me to pray. But
those words of long ago lie like burnt-out cinders in my hand
and there is no life in them anymore. They simply have no
relevance for *me*. And so I am excluded from those fortunate
ones who find the mysterious gate and can feel that those bells
are ringing for them. I would like to have that peace that was
so real to my foxhole buddy, the man who shared my hunger in

the prisoner-of-war camp, the woman with whom I went through the terrors of the bombings; these people radiate an atmosphere of courage and security. How glad I'd be to live in that peace. But it's not for me. And when in church the minister says, "Peace be with you," I think I know what that could mean, but I can't reach out for it, because peace doesn't reach out for me. Perhaps I'm just one of those people who will never find the gate, one of the many who have a different fate.

All right, then listen to the message of this text. The very fact that Jesus is saying to you right here and now, "Strive to enter by the narrow door" and you are hearing it now means that it is open to you. And all that you are asked is whether you are willing to fight until you die, whether you are really in earnest, whether for you this is more than mere yearning or Faustian infatuation with a bit of searching for the truth. The door is open to you, because you are hearing Jesus' words. Or do you think he is a mere juggler, trying to make a fool of you? Do you think he is a cynic, playing a game of cat-and-mouse with you, luring you on, only to slam the door in your face? You would be taking the Son of God for a devil, if that's what you assume, if you do not have the desire to run to him and cast his promises at his feet, saying: you promised, you said it; now here I am; I'm yours!

Our text closes with the somber picture of the falling of night, the night when no man can work, the hour when the door is locked and the great midnight of the world is come. For Jesus can say, not only what he said at the marriage in Cana, "My hour has not yet come," but also, "My hour is past; the time has run out." But because we think we have "forever," we don't like to think about that.

Then the great silence will descend upon the world. The preachers, if there are any left, will move about the chancels like mute shadows; but the Word will sound forth no more, for the power and the Spirit will have vanished and the acceptable time will be over. The hands of the preachers will point toward the heavens, but where the heavens were there will be only a storm cloud and "seated on the cloud one like a man." And the world will say: the hour of Christendom is past and new gods will begin to inhabit the throne of heaven. But the truth will be just the opposite; for then the hour of the *world* will be past and the time of its visitation will be over.

In the face of this dreadful possibility we ask once more: Has this hour already elapsed? Has the passing shower of the gospel long since passed over Germany and the blessed cloud already disappeared beyond the horizon? Do we not hear those pain-filled words of Jesus, spoken over our country and perhaps over this whole world which is shaken by the winds and woes of the last times: "Would that even today you knew the things that make for peace! But now they are hid from your eyes"? Have not the bombing raids, the terrors of the collapse, the thunders of battle, the miseries of the displaced passed over and left everything just as it was before? So we ask, is the hour past already? Are not the last sirens already screaming? Is not the midnight hour already plunging in upon us, that last hour of which Georges Bernanos, the French writer, spoke in his famous novel, *The Diary of a Country Priest:* "But just you wait. Wait for the first quarter-of-an-hour's silence. Then the Word will be heard of men—not the voice they rejected, which spoke so quietly: 'I am the Way, the Resurrection and the Life'—but the voice from the depths: 'I am the door for ever locked, the road which leads nowhere, the lie, the everlasting dark'"?

But still, contrary to all expectation, he did *not* say, "Would that you had *known*." Still he is saying "Would that *even today you* knew the things that make for peace!" There is still time; the hour is still here and the Word is being preached, the message of Jesus, "Strive to enter" is still being heard! Still he goes through the land with blessing in his hands, still he is the open door. But we enter now as God's hand is already on the latch and the last trumpets are being raised. Twelve—this is the goal of time. O man, remember eternity.

So even this glimpse of falling night is not meant to mislead us into melancholy. "What's the use?"—anybody who says that does not understand the mystery of the last aeon. No, the nearness of the midnight hour rouses us to make the final effort, to accept the final orders. It sends us out once more into the streets to cry out again: Lord, stay with us, for it is toward evening and the day is now far spent!

We live in the time of the last appeal. This night the Lord will be asking for your soul. Where are you? Where do you stand? Tonight, this night!

15

The Foundation of Life

"Every one then who hears these words of mine and does them will
be like a wise man who built his house upon the rock; and the rain
fell, and the floods came, and the winds blew and beat upon that
house, but it did not fall, because it had been founded on the rock.
And everyone who hears these words of mine and does not do them
will be like a foolish man who built his house upon the sand; and the
rain fell, and the floods came, and the winds blew and beat against
that house, and it fell; and great was the fall of it."

                                                —*Matthew 7:24-27*

Every one of us wants to be a wise man and every one of us
would like to build the house of his life properly.

So when Jesus speaks of these two wishes which are common
to all of us he is really addressing *every* man. Hitherto he has
been speaking chiefly to the disciples. But now as he begins
to speak about wisdom and a man's own house, even the people
in the back row suddenly prick up their ears. He is saying
that a man can handle his life, his business, his job wisely and
sensibly, or he can do all this foolishly, ineptly, and clumsily.
It is colossally stupid, for example, for a man to put thousands
of dollars into building the facade and interior decoration of his
house and forget the simplest prerequisite, that is, to find out
whether the ground on which it is built is sound. Otherwise,
even the finest mansion will come down around his ears. A

man is a fool if he allows his own stupidity to bury him under his own house. A man is a fool who throws his money away for things that cannot function and on the other hand economizes where he ought to be liberal and especially careful, because this is the main thing, namely, the foundations.

"What this man up front is saying," think these two, "really sounds quite sensible. He actually has his feet on the ground and isn't floating around in the clouds. And apparently he knows something about architecture—about the practical architecture of life. Obviously he means that this God he is always talking about not only has something to do with being religious and believing in the life to come but also with the question of whether one deals 'wisely' with life, with getting on in *this* life, or whether one acts like a fool and gets wrecked because he neglects the most important thing."

Well, what does this man up front mean by this "house" he is talking about? He obviously means the house of our life. All of us are building upon this house, and others are helping us at it. Our mother's love carried the first stones for the building when she brought us into the world and strove to keep us strong and healthy. The first sounds of our speech we learned from her, and it was she who first taught us to fold our hands in prayer. It was our mothers who built love into the walls of our life from the beginning. Without love these walls would certainly never have been raised.

And then we had to go on building ourselves. We went to school, we shouldered the first responsibilities, and we were told that we must do this and do that or we would never amount to anything. So we began ourselves to gather stones for the house of our life, at first small, individual ones with weak childish hands (a few plain maxims and the ABC's) and finally great loads carried now on the stronger shoulders of grown men and women. We perhaps had some joy and pride as we succeeded here and there, learning that the boss was satisfied with what we accomplished, doing a good job in our trade, filling our place as a merchant, or sowing and harvesting love as the mother in a home. How many people, parents, friends, comrades, contributed to the building of this house of our life and making it what it is now!

But there are pits and gaps in the masonry too. There were reverses and hard times when not much progress was made. There were faulty constructions and wrong estimates. But anyhow, our life is a house—perhaps a mansion with respectable doors and a garden and an impressive atmosphere, perhaps a small and miserable hovel. But however that may be, we live in it and we try to keep our house weather-tight and be secure within it.

And we succeed, for a time. But into every life there come storms, when suddenly the question of the condition of the foundations and the cellars becomes acute. Then all at once one sees his house from an altogether different point of view. In peaceful times one takes a simple delight in the comfort of the living room, the fine view, and everything that has really turned out well in one's life: the fact that we are making a living, that we enjoy our work, and get along well with our friends and neighbors. But then suddenly there is a war, the sirens scream, the Christmas trees appear in the sky, and fire and brimstone rain down. Then the question of the cellars and foundations comes to the fore. Then all at once it is no longer important whether the house of our life is spick and span and comfortable and whether it is looked upon with approval—all this could be swept away in a second. Then everything depends upon whether it is sound and secure in the depths and whether one can find shelter there. Then perhaps that shabby monster of a house in the neighborhood is far better because it has this reliability in its depths and foundations. Then perhaps that man who was thought to be rather plain and reserved and never made much of himself, who was hardly noticed by his neighbors and whose friendship nobody sought, perhaps this man with the homely facade suddenly turns out to be a man who stands strangely secure in the hour of disaster, a man who radiates an encouraging and sustaining power upon those around him, so that many find in him a pillar of strength—even the man in the neighborhood with the attractive home of his own, which has long since been swept away by the storm of bombs, and now is so helpless as he hangs suspended over the abyss of nothingness.

We have all experienced something like that, for our generation is one that has come through great storms and is even now moving toward horizons threatened with heavy, black clouds. And for many of *us* our houses have collapsed—and not only houses of stone and wood, but rather the houses of our lives.

There, for example, is the refugee from the East. He had to leave house and home and all his possessions. Do you realize what that means, the old chest of drawers that belonged to great-grandmother, the familiar creak in the steps, the patter of rain in the big barrel, the neatly arranged linen closet, filled with the work of diligent hands over decades and always fragrant with the faint odor of lavender, and all the many little things, utterable and unutterable, that go to make up the sweet scent and atmosphere of home? And now it's utterly gone. And perhaps for the exile the collapse of all these things has meant the collapse of the house of his own life. What is left, apart from all these things, to make life worth living? Is there any ground that has not been shaken and shattered? Is there a place where one can go on existing meaningfully, a place where one can "be" something and count for something—quite *independent* of the house and home and wife and child, which are destroyed, lost, or dead—a place where one can be safe and happy despite all this?

You see, here again is the question of the foundations of the house of life that Jesus points to in this text. Never before did the refugee think when he rose from his own bed and looked up to the sky and when at night he turned out the light in the familiar room that one day he would ask, would be *compelled* to ask that question, and that then everything would depend on some things in life which were altogether different from those with which he was concerned hour by hour and day by day.

Take General Harras in Zuckmayer's play *The Devil's General.* Now there was a "real guy," full of radiant vitality; everybody liked him. And what a wonderful, jolly life it is to be "at home" in such an atmosphere of sympathy and enthusiasm! What a feeling of security to be "at home" in the hearts of many people who loved you, indeed, of people who idolize you and would go through fire for you! This is really to have a "house in the sun." And above all, General Harras was consumed with his passion for flying. Anybody who has ever been above the clouds knows what a glorious, beautiful, thrilling thing flying can be. And we understand then why General Harras set his heart on becoming a flier and a general in the air force, no matter who he flew for and who he fought for—even if it was for the devil. His house was the air, the wild blue yonder, his marvelous, exultant vitality.

And all of a sudden the storms come into his life too. He sees what is happening to the Jews. He sees the injustice and the brutality and all the dark shadows, which I need not conjure up here, because we have all lived in them. And General Harras was hopelessly delivered over to them, because he had sold his soul to the *master* of these shadows, because it was from him that he had received his plane, his uniforms, the spacious skies, and the good companions in whose hearts he lived. Suddenly he was faced with the hardest question of all: Is your accomplishment, is this satisfaction you find in your profession, is the good companionship you have with your fellow workers, is all this really a "house" in which you can live, a house that can survive the hurricanes of life? Have you not forgotten, General Harras, the question of what kind of *ground* you built upon? Have you forgotten that you—with all your brilliant life—may not have settled down in a muddy swamp? Perhaps you have really overlooked the question of *whom* it is you are working for, in *whose* name you are willing to live and die. Did the question never occur to you—in the play a young officer who is fanatically devoted to him timidly suggests this to him in the last, darkest hours—whether you have reckoned your life without your host, whether you have left out the main factor, God, so that you end up serving the devil? "Do you believe in God, General?" Then the shadows swallowed him up. The plane, which once bore him up so gloriously, threw him out; the air, into whose heady expanses he hurled himself so joyously, let him fall; and not only the machine, which lay on the ground a smoking wreck, but he himself, his life, his brilliant career, the fine uniform and the decorations were a wreck. It had all been an empty, insubstantial nothing.

Well, it is the same catastrophe that has befallen countless numbers of us, people who tried to accomplish the best, who wanted to do decent work in the military, in social affairs, or as teachers, perhaps even as politicians, and even had some success and satisfaction, people who thought they had erected a solid house in which they could live their lives—and yet made only *one* mistake. And that mistake was their failure to ask in *whose* name they were doing this, *whose* wagon they were pulling. Or perhaps it was a mother who raised her children with love and many sacrifices, who went hungry in order to feed them, wore shabby clothes in order that they might be neatly dressed, and yet depriving them of the ultimate foundations of life or even giving them false goals—with one hand giving them the goods of this world (food and drink, clothing, and shoes) and with the other depriving them of the world to come. The point is that in the last analysis the important thing in life is not whether a man, or a woman, has a bright mind, but rather *which* light it is that makes this brightness, whether it is the light of eternity or the sulphurous light of Satan, in other words, whether he turns out to be the devil's general. It is not a matter of whether he is a strong fellow with sufficient energy and ambition, or whether he has both feet on the ground, but rather of *what* ground he is standing on. If the ground gives way, even the strongest legs are of no use to him; for then the stronger he is the more quickly will he entangle himself in the brambles and the swamp.

And that gives us a bead on the point in our life to which Jesus is pointing, namely, that point at which the *foundation* of our life is at stake.

He tells us that this foundation is the Word of God which a man hears and does.

What does this mean?

That the Word of God is a foundation that lies beneath the zone where the storms rage and provides us with a place of shelter is shown by the fact that there is not a single stage in our life where we will be obliged to abandon it because it is not relevant. We can have the greatest respect for Goethe's *Faust* and Shakespeare's plays, and they may have set off some grand and stimulating storms in our life. But would you read these things to cancer patients in a hospital ward? Would these works be suitable in the spiritual climate of a crowd of refugees or the mass burials after the great bombing raids? Obviously, these are words for the peaks and pinnacles of the house of life; but they cannot be the foundations that will sustain and preserve us in the storms of meaninglessness, mass deaths, hunger, and the frantic fear of life and the future.

But the Word of the Lord—and Jesus Christ himself *is* this Word—is relevant at every station of life. It is there at the cradle and the grave. It is there when wedding bells ring, and it is there in the night of suffering. It sounded forth its "Let

there be" on the morning of creation, and it will be the Word
that will not pass away when heaven and earth pass away and
are toppled into the great grave of the universe.

It is there, always there. It is there with its blessing even
before we understand it, when it is spoken at the cradle, in baptism, and in our mother's prayers. And when we grow to consciousness we find that already it is there. And when we prepare for our last hour, when we no longer feel the touch of the
beloved hand that cannot let us go, when our dreams dissolve
and those we love are left behind on the hither shore, when the
songs of birds are silenced and the sun goes dark, then, even
then, this Word does not desert us; now it imbues with substance
the prayer of bygone days: "When I depart, depart thou not
from me." No, it does not depart; it comes to meet us on the
other shore. Any pastor who deals with the dying learns again
and again that these words penetrate to levels and depths that
no human words can reach. They are the last companions as we
cross the unknown border, and they are the first to greet us on
the other side, where they are still true and valid.

And then too, this Word is present in the happy hours of our
life. It blesses the meager and the rich meal, and it weeps with
those who weep; it gives life in death, riches in poverty, hope
in hopelessness. And how could it be otherwise, since all our
ways, that lead us through a thousand stations of suffering and
joy, hope and despondency, must finally end at the throne of
God, that throne from which this Word came forth and at
which it now finds its final triumph and fulfillment? How could
it be otherwise, when at every one of these stations there awaits
us that *One*, who wept with the widow of Nain and allowed her
grief to tremble through his own heart, who shared the merriment of the celebrators at the wedding at Cana, and dies the
death of all who die?

And all this gives us a picture of *why* it is that the Word of
God is the foundation of life. It is, simply because it is abiding,

because it is faithful and true, because there is not a moment in life when it is not relevant and valid. Not a single moment; neither the hour of guilt, when it judges me and grants me forgiveness, nor the hour in which meaninglessness of fierce disasters beats down upon me; for then it speaks of those higher thoughts that are planning our life and comforts our faith with the promise of all that we shall one day be permitted to see.

Heaven and earth will pass away—and so, too, will everything else with which heaven and earth has comforted and sustained us, everything else with which they have tormented, confused, and tempted us. So even Faust's shining tracks will disappear in this aeon,* and Shakespeare's Richard III and all the blood-stained murderers and tormentors of history will be forgotten, and fair Helen will be lost to memory. The loveliest evening songs—

> O'er all the hilltops
> Is quiet now,
> In all the treetops
> Hearest thou
> Hardly a breath. . .

—will die away, because the treetops and hilltops, whose evening stillness they extol, lie on this side of the great divide that then will wall this burnt-out world. Yes, heaven and earth will pass away—*but his words will not pass away*. And therefore those will not pass away who have lived and died by this Word and desired to be on the side of him who spoke this Word and was himself this Word:

> Through sin and death he strides,
> Through this world's grief he rides,
> He strides through hell's dark tide;
>   Where'er he goes,
>   I too abide.
> He keeps me by his side.

* [The allusion is to Faust's boast, "The traces of my earthly being / Can perish not in aeons"; Goethe, *Faust*, Part II, Act V. TRANS.]

That's why the Word of God is the rock foundation that defies the storms. And therefore it is not shifting sand that washes away. But then Jesus adds another important clause. It is not the Word of God as such that becomes this rock foundation for us, but only the Word of God that we *do*, the Word that we take seriously in our life. And therefore it is not the words we rattle off daily as we mechanically say grace at table, nor is it a hurried recitation of the Lord's Prayer or our daily Bible reading. All this may well be thrown with all the rest upon the rubbish heap of this transient world; it may rise up to accuse us as the Word of God we have murdered and desecrated. No; the only Word that abides to eternity is the Word that is *done*.

What does it mean to "do" the Word of God?

It means quite simply to *live* with this Word. It means first of all to take seriously the reality of the cares in my life, the very real concern as to how I can get through a financial crisis, how I can make out with my small pension, where I can take refuge if the worst comes to the worst. I say that to live with this Word means to take seriously the reality of all these cares, but then to let the Word of God be an even *greater* reality. It means to take seriously the Word that says that tomorrow, which I worry about so much, is safe in the hands of God, that nothing can happen to me except what he has foreseen and scrutinized, and that "in everything God works for good," for my good, if I let him take charge of my life and do not let my love grow cold.

To "live" with this Word means quite simply to dare to be obedient, even where humanly speaking it seems foolish to be obedient; to tell the truth when it is dangerous or "stupid" to tell the truth, but where God really demands that it be spoken—and then with all your heart trust that God will not let you down, but will make his promises come true.

To "live" with this Word means accepting whatever falls to my lot—the friend who is having a hard time of it, the letter of condolence that I must write, the business transaction I have to carry out, the wonderful clear, cold autumn air I breathe on a week end, the conference in the Kremlin I read about in the newspapers, the fever of my sick child, the illness of my neighbor, the toil of my job, the rest and peace of a day off—and take all this to God in prayer and supplication and thanksgiving. Then I am "doing" the Word, then I am "building" upon it.

It's true all right that the Word of God is a rock foundation on which I can build my life. But then it's also true that now I must anchor, fasten, and moor this Word of God in every situation of my life, in everything, absolutely everything, that is important to me. Do you think this Word can become my companion and friend, my rod and staff, if I hear it on Sundays or read it in the morning and then go on my way—as if my neighbor's illness had only to do with medical science, as if the conference in the Kremlin were only a political matter, as if all of this were not completely and exclusively grounded in and governed by him who can turn the hearts of men wherever he wills as he does the rivers of water, who can command the storms, restore the sick, wake the dead, and transform burdens and cares into pure blessings?

The only Word that is rock foundation is the Word that you really stand upon.

I know, it sounds paradoxical, but it is true. The Word of God *seems* to be sand. Isn't it a terribly risky thing to stake one's life on a thing that is so "unverifiable," concerning itself with myths and prehistory instead of relying upon what is nearest at hand, upon fists and elbows, instinct, and common sense? Well, for him who thinks in this way the Word *is* nothing more than sand. For him who takes it merely as an "extra" in his life (a little religion, a little worship, a little note of sad eternity now and then makes a man feel better!), for him it drifts away like sand, and the first good storm will blow away what is left of his sand-Christianity. How many sand-Christians, nominal Christians were blasted by the storm of the war, stripped, like a tree of its leaves, of the little bits of faith they still carried, only to go on vegetating as barren nihilists reduced to mortal poverty!

But for him who dares to *stand* upon it, who simply takes the risk of living with Jesus Christ, this seeming sand suddenly stiffens into rock on which he can stand in utter confidence, laughing at the storms and winds, because they are the breath of the voice of God, because this very voice of God, that makes the earth to tremble and the mountains to smoke, has called him by name, because it is God's rock that keeps him standing and God's hand that holds him safe.

He who is safe in eternity need no longer fear what time brings. He who has the peace that passes all understanding no longer needs to fear the specters of terrible future possibilities conjured up by his mind. He who knows that he is loved no longer kills himself in hating other men. He who serves the Prince of Life is no longer the slave of death. He who hears above him the song of angels, rejoicing because he has found his way home to the Father's joy, is no longer afraid of the war cries of the nations. He who knows him who overcame the world has escaped the specters. He who trusts the hand that rules the "ends of the earth" knows that even *his* poor, guilty life is being safely led through all the woes of dying, the grave, and the darkness of death to the Last Day and the Father's throne, where every tear will be dried and there shall be no mourning, no crying, and no more death, but only the song of the redeemed: Enter into the joy of your Lord!

When we live in the name of his last homecoming, prepared for us by Jesus Christ, and when in the name of this last homecoming we look upon every pain and joy that may come to us as a visitation and a preparation for that day, then we know that every storm can only drive us toward that haven and that even the darkest roads through the valley of the shadow can lead only to the gates of the Father's house. And that means that we can withstand any storm, simply because we are upheld by *him* who abides for ever, the Alpha and the Omega, and from whose hand nothing can snatch us.

Let this be the praise with which we close these meditations on the Sermon on the Mount: He, Jesus Christ, is the rock on which I stand, the hand that will never let me go, the eternity that abides, the peace that holds within its grasp all the strife of this world—as a father holds the hands of his feverish child.

And when Jesus finished these sayings, the crowds were astonished at his teaching, for he taught them as one who had authority, and not as their scribes.

Type used in this book
Body, 10 on 13 and 9 on 11 Janson
Display, Tempo
Paper: White Antique "R"